Getting IT

of related interest

Coming Out Asperger
Diagnosis, Disclosure and Self-Confidence
Edited by Dinah Murray
ISBN 1 84310 240 4

Finding You Finding Me
**Using Intensive Interaction to get in touch with people whose severe
learning disabilities are combined with autistic spectrum disorder**
Phoebe Caldwell
ISBN 1 84310 399 0

Succeeding with Interventions for Asperger Syndrome Adolescents
A Guide to Communication and Socialisation in Interaction Therapy
John Harpur, Maria Lawlor and Michael Fitzgerald
ISBN 184310 322 2

Survival Strategies for People on the Autism Spectrum
Marc Fleisher
ISBN 1 84310 261 7

Quality of Life and Disability
An Approach for Community Practitioners
Ivan Brown and Roy I. Brown
Foreword by Ann and Rud Turnbull
ISBN 1 84310 005 3

Getting IT

Using Information Technology to Empower People with Communication Difficulties

Dinah Murray and Ann Aspinall

Jessica Kingsley Publishers
London and Philadelphia

First published in 2006
by Jessica Kingsley Publishers
116 Pentonville Road
London N1 9JB, UK
and
400 Market Street, Suite 400
Philadelphia, PA 19106, USA

www.jkp.com

Library of Congress Cataloging in Publication Data
Murray, Dinah, 1946-
 Getting IT : using information technology to empower people with communication difficul-
ties / Dinah Murray and Ann Aspinall.-- 1st paperback ed.
  p. cm.
 Includes bibliographical references and index.
 ISBN-13: 978-1-84310-375-2 (pbk. : alk. paper)
 ISBN-10: 1-84310-375-3 (pbk. : alk. paper) 1. Computers and people with disabilities. 2.
Assistive computer technology--Design. 3. Microcomputers--Social aspects. I. Aspinall, Ann,
1946- II. Title.
 HV1569.5.M87 2006
 681'.761--dc22

                                                    2006000872

British Library Cataloguing in Publication Data
A CIP catalogue record for this book is available from the British Library

ISBN-13: 978 1 84310 375 2
ISBN-10: 1 84310 375 3

Printed and bound in Great Britain by
Athenaeum Press, Gateshead, Tyne and Wear

Contents

Introduction

About Getting IT

We know that people who do not speak can amaze people with their articulacy at the keyboard. We know people who find it hard to communicate or make friends in the real world but construct real friendships online. In the real world where you can see and hear each other, people are impatient for articulation and meaningful response and see unusual movements as a reason to dismiss and disregard you; you are constantly bombarded with information you can't switch off; everyone else is in an unintelligible and unpredictable rush. At the computer people are safe from the impact of society's rejection of the slow and odd. At the computer people who do not speak have a voice.

This book is meant to inspire people to use information technology (IT) with people in care and expand the skills and knowledge of those already doing so. In the next chapter we describe the impact IT has had on the lives of actual people the authors have known. Between us we have worked for about 30 years with people who have learning and/or communication disabilities of various kinds. We ourselves have been excited and inspired when we have seen how access to IT can transform people's lives. How to use information technology to make voices heard is the essential theme of this book.

With the help of that great bit of software, the businessman's friend, Microsoft PowerPoint (hereafter referred to as PowerPoint), anyone can make an impressive personal presentation. It is a very powerful tool that is very easy to use. This book has a whole lot of ideas about how to use it in a wide variety of ways to empower and enrich the lives of people with communication issues of various sorts. In the middle section, Chapters 2 to 8, we tell the story of three imaginary people in care who benefit from IT. Everything that happens in the lives our three heroes has in fact happened to real people. Much of it could happen with anyone, even people who do not read or write.

It is delightful to be able to expand PowerPoint's user base and turn it into a tool of empowerment and inclusion. Ann Aspinall of the Home Farm Trust has been using the programme or its predecessors in just this way for many years now among what is often the most excluded of populations, people with learning disabilities. Used correctly it can generate a liberating confidence in people who have never felt 'able' before. At the same time, staff who have been involved in introducing the information technology – and may themselves have received just a few hours of basic training – are also empowered and liberated by it (see Aspinall and Hegarty 2001 for more about this). Like Ann, Dinah Murray has hands-on experience of using PowerPoint and IT in general with a range of people who are receiving paid care, many but not all of whom are on the autism spectrum.

To some extent the contents of the book reflect the two authors' chance preferences about software and websites. For example, you may prefer a different picture display website to the one used here, you may prefer a different search engine to Google, and so on. The ideas in this book aren't generally restricted to running on our preferred software, and readers may have their own favourite programmes for carrying out what are basically the same operations. Most of the advice we give is equally applicable to Apple Macs and PCs with Windows operating systems. When we know about a significant difference we tell you about it. There are references to using both software and hardware throughout the text and some light advice about how to do that. These references are backed up in the last section of the book, Chapters 9 and 10.

The book falls into three sections. This and the next chapter form an introduction to the issues around using information technology with people in care which are played out in the central (semi-fictional) section. Inclusion in the twenty-first century – much hyped as a desirable practice in decent sounding legislation around the world – must involve access to the full range of information and communication technology that has empowered and liberated so many. The next chapter presents two strands of argument in support of this case.

One strand of the argument in Chapter 1 is presented in the shape of a series of case studies. These are of real people making real achievements through their experiences with information technology. Difficulties with communicating their needs and wants have dogged their lives. Often in the past they have been treated as people who have nothing to say because they cannot speak. Now their lives have been turned around because they have found ways to get their messages across. This strand is a series of vignettes drawn from Ann's rich experience of using information and communication technology with service users in the Home Farm Trust. Every one of these tales should persuade you that even people who need high levels of support can achieve much in this way. They can access enriching experiences, they can present themselves with style, they can receive new respect. Above all, they can communicate effectively.

The other strand of argument in Chapter 1 is a general discussion of the ethical and legal case for ensuring that everyone in care has full access to IT and we have included a number of case studies to support this case. The discussion focuses on 'joining up' government thinking to show that meeting legal requirements concerning providing adequate services to people in care must involve providing them with access to the information technology which in the twenty-first century penetrates every other corner of life.

The white paper Valuing People (Department of Health 2001) forcefully introduced the idea of person-centred planning (PCP) into thinking about provision for people with learning disabilities. It suggests that without a PCP process in place for all those people who are entitled to care, the further aims and purposes of government policy will be unattainable. We suggest that the PCP process itself and the other goals of 'rights, independence, choice and inclusion' can all be much advantaged through the use of IT. We suggest that it is a farce to talk about inclusion in particular without addressing the issues of limited or non-existent access to IT in this population.

The other main source of government thinking discussed in Chapter 2 is proposed legislation about mental capacity. We applaud the Law Society's advice which underpins the coming legislation which makes it clear that certain steps must be taken to maximise any individual's capacity to make decisions before delegating or devolving such capacity to another person. We suggest further that taking those steps should in most cases involve deploying information technology since it can have a great impact on the capacity to store, recall, and access information relevant to decisions of any sort. These capacities are essential to decision making. IT can also play a key role in enabling decisions to be communicated. In addition, we propose that observing both human rights legislation and disability discrimination legislation equally implies that service providers should ensure universal access to IT, including the Internet, email, printers, scanners and cameras. We are hopeful that forthcoming social care legislation in the UK will have taken these rather obvious arguments on board and will build in a requirement to provide such access.

The bulk of the book, from Chapter 2 to Chapter 8, is made up of the stories of three fictional people. The three narratives which weave through this section illustrate the great variety of ways information and communication technology can benefit people who need a bit of help in their lives. With that help such people may be able to make valuable contributions themselves. A bonus for service providers is that people who are leading fulfilling lives and making contact with the outside world are much less likely to become stressed, anxious or angry. They are much less likely to do things that upset other people and are regarded as 'challenging'. Please note we are *not* arguing that access to information technology is a substitute for personal support – everyone needs real people around. We are, however, saying that it is likely in the long run to reduce staff costs by reducing the frequency of situations which call for extra 'defensive' staff – the main reason why challenging behaviours are such a drain on resources. Empowering service users in this way may turn out to be a very cost-effective strategy. An added benefit of reducing their 'challenging behaviours' for service users is that it may bring them freedom from the sort of constant surveillance they often suffer.

Service users who pose a real challenge to provision are often identified as autistic, or as belonging somewhere on the autism spectrum, or as having autistic traits. Autistic people often report that knowing how to get out is a key issue for them whenever they are indoors. They also often report that they do not like to be watched and/or that they can't cope with more than one person at a time. It doesn't take much imagination to appreciate how bad it must make such people feel to be incarcerated and subjected to non-stop scrutiny. Making people feel bad and reducing their freedom is not a good way to avoid problematic behaviour! Giving people access to ways of communicating hands them power and increases their freedom.

Two of our central characters are on the autism spectrum, one, Kumar, is very verbal – even verbose on occasion – while the other, Irene, has never been known to speak. Our third character, Marie, is a woman who has had a full and active life until recently, but now finds that her short-term memory problems are too severe for her to manage daily life without support. She had never used a computer before the events in this book. Although her background is so different from that of the others, a computer's predictability and structure and the visible on-screen presence of prompts are as pleasing to her as they are to the other two.

Each of our heroes discovers ways in which information technology enhances their power over what happens in their own lives and enables them to make new connections with other people. Kumar, the man with an autistic spectrum disorder (ASD), has real expertise in computing; his main, and severe, problems are with actual people and real life. In this book we see how in the twenty-first century engaging with life via computers may be a huge social blessing for someone who needs more time than most to process social meaning. Attitudes and perceptions about a person's competence and intelligence tend to be strongly influenced by their ability to communicate with you. Information technology puts everyone on a 'level playing field' for communication.

Neither non-speaking Irene nor Marie with her failing memory is a very obvious person to introduce to computing. Neither of them is young, neither of them has any previous hands-on experience of computers: they both need to be persuaded this is something they can do and want to do! In their different ways, they are both motivated to engage with computers by the use of non-verbal material.

All sorts of aspects of using IT come up as the stories of our protagonists unfold in this book. In these stories we have mainly drawn on software and hardware that is commonly available and inexpensive; only Irene uses some adaptive 'assistive technology'. The technical chapter which concludes the book provides an overview of more specialist technology. Every event we describe in the narrative chapters, except Chapter 8, has happened to someone in real life – we have compressed events from a lot of different lives to make the lives of our heroes. The only events we have purely imagined are those in Chapter 8, in which we have ventured to create a bit of science fiction. The technology we envisage there is only in the pipeline at the time of writing this book, but we are hopeful that it will become a reality before the book is dust.

We create lifestories using Powerpoint. We use scanners and cameras and sound recording. We make presentations on a variety of topics in a variety of styles for a variety of reasons. We encounter emails and email groups, later on we encounter blogs and blog rings. We use video in a lot of different ways, including analysing and reflecting on the best way to present a case. We apply the principles of self-advocacy and take the necessary steps to promote it and the person-centred planning process, using IT. We discuss motivating people to use IT. We look into ways of using pictures to communicate and promote choice. We explore the benefits of Widgit Rebus symbols versus the benefits of writing, we look at text-to-speech devices and programmes. We mull over issues around programming a communication board. We investigate a variety of ways of using the Internet for research, recreation and activism. We consider using printers to make statements, T-shirts and business cards. We touch on issues around Internet security and restrictive access. We show how setting up meetings and organising a fair vote can be aided by judicious use of IT. In the sci-fi chapter (Chapter 8) which concludes the narrative section we look at possible developments and blends of PDAs, mobiles and cameras. All three of our heroes have far less dead time on their hands by the end of the story! And they have all made real connections with real people. This is not about using computers to escape from the world, it is about using them to connect with it.

All of those encounters with IT happen in the natural course of events in the stories we tell in the middle section which forms the bulk of this book. In the final section, Chapters 9 and 10 which are about how to get IT right, we go into more technical detail. Chapter 9, 'Taking Control of Time', sets out the steps for creating an interactive calendar using PowerPoint. If you follow these steps you will make a really useful template which can be used by anyone. You will also learn a great deal about how to get the most out of PowerPoint as you work your way through it. The next chapter is about using the technology and provides an overview of the many ways technology has been adapted to suit people with specific difficulties. This chapter and the appendices which follow it are solidly practical and can be treated as self-standing. That is, if you don't like fiction, and you don't think you need inspiring, you could use this part of the book on its own. It is intended as a resource. Equally, if you have a great grasp of the technology, but are stuck for ways of using it creatively, you could skip the technical section and just read the story for the ideas it may give you. The appendices cover tips for small-scale processes which have been noted throughout the narrative; helpsheets for lengthier more complex processes; a list of resources which includes organisations and contacts; and references to articles, books and websites mentioned in the text.

With these tools we can change the world.

Chapter 1

Inclusion in the Twenty-first Century

The Argument for Ensuring IT Access

Many of the problems which arise when one is attempting to include people with disabilities adequately in society can be at least partially solved through the use of IT. In this chapter we look at some of these problems and how IT can help, and tell the stories of some of the people with whom we have worked whose lives have been radically improved by the introduction of IT.

Identifying and accessing relevant information

People who have difficulties with decision making are likely to need sensitive support at the initial stage of identifying what information is needed, and constructive support in accessing it. The narrow focus of interest which is typical for people on the autistic spectrum can mean that even the most apparently able people with the condition may miss relevant connections and implications. Relevant information must include advice about potential outcomes, since these are unlikely to be obvious to people with ASDs.

For instance, at the library or with friends, we can bring our understanding of a wide range of issues to bear in working out what specific information we need, and how to find it out. With little effort we access phone and phone directories, Yellow Pages and other classified directories, and can find the right headings under which to search; we think of the right questions to ask and the right people of whom to ask them. Few people with learning disabilities are likely to have the background education, the confidence, or the opportunities to enable such effective informal research. We all use the Internet, too, of course; Google has become one of our best friends – 'anyone can Google'. With a bit of help in identifying what to search for, there is no reason why people with learning disabilities, autism, dementia or of problematic capacity for any other reason shouldn't also be able to use Google, or other similar search engines. If you know how to find it, all information found electronically can be digitally stored and accessed later.

The need for a calm and supportive emotional climate

Nobody is likely to make good decisions when they feel under pressure. Other people's questions and expectations are inherently pressurising: considered reflection might be more effective without that pressure. Having all the information available in searchable form at home, e.g. on a computer, so that it can be revisited as often as needed, will contribute to the chances of a calm emotional climate for decision making. Not being under time pressure is also vital, not just for adequate processing to take place, but also to maintain emotional calm.

Understanding information relevant to the decision

Clear effective communication from whomever is providing support will be crucial to ensure good understanding of relevant information. Information will need to be plainly and carefully stated, using assistive communication when required, and it will need to be fully explicit and not assume background knowledge. Sufficient processing time must be given to the recipient; and information must be given in a written or graphic form in which it can be revisited as often as necessary.

Retaining information relevant to the decision

Everyone needs help retaining information: notes, photos, ground-plans: objects of various sorts which store information, files, folders, cardboard boxes or – best of all – computers. An easy-to-open, easily browsed file with all the relevant information plainly set out in it can be placed on a computer Desktop so that it is also easy to find. It can be opened any time for consideration and re-consideration: the information is both preserved and accessible, i.e. it is effectively retained.

Using relevant information

This occurs naturally once the information has been identified, acquired and stored for the purpose of making the decision, as above. Once it has been accessed and accessibly retained, information will be used so long as the individual who is being assisted in the process of making the decision has understood both the information and its relevance: to grasp its relevance is to use it.

Communicating that decision

Communicating that decision (whether by talking, using sign language *or any other means*) will only be possible if one is accessing a recognised and accepted mode of communication. When communication problems are prominent, special steps must be taken to ensure information flow. In some cases, with sufficiently supportive and sensitive care, communication may be far from standard and yet highly effective.

However, the more broadly accepted a means of communication is, the greater its potential social and communicative power. Speech is the main currency of social exchange, so people who are not able to deploy speech are *de facto* excluded from many social situations; their views are likely to be devalued just because those views depend on another person to turn them into social currency. However, information technology is emotionally and socially neutral, and universally accessible in principle. For examples of the sensitive and constructive use of IT in helping people to acquire the ability to communicate their choices effectively, please take a look at the case studies in this chapter. At a computer, people who find the rapid exchange of speech impossibly demanding may be able to function as well as or better than most people. Anecdotal evidence (see *inter alia* www.autistics.org debate about Applied Behaviour Analysis (ABA), an intensive behaviour modification system), as well as the most recent research into facilitated communication (Grayson 2004), suggests that many people who do not speak *do* read, and can express their views effectively with a keyboard. For those who prefer or are used to dealing with visual symbols such as Widgit's Rebus (www.widgit.com) there is a variety of software, including email software which will translate from symbols to text and vice versa.

Since according to the diagnostic criteria autism is a communicative disability, failing to provide accessible and acceptable modes of communication including email may well be discriminatory in service provision for people on the autism spectrum. People with other learning issues and people with senile dementia typically also have communication difficulties. IT can contribute in many ways to individual autonomy, having the potential to find, store, retrieve and display relevant information about people's personal histories, relationships, goals and interests in a way which those people can control. Computers and their peripherals offer great possibilities for building up a store of treasured, easily shareable, images. Access to email means people can exchange messages and pictures with family and friends with minimum effort.

As always, there are potential undesirable consequences, some of which can easily be foreseen and managed. The equipment must be preserved for service users and adequate provision of IT for staff use is also necessary. Staff working in the context of good management practices will usually have access to an office computer. The equipment will also need to be maintained. Another possibility is that service users will access chatrooms and/or seek out pornography. We would advocate that such use should be monitored but not prevented unless a service user is pursuing matters of serious concern such as suicide or illegal sexual activity. It may sometimes be necessary to intervene, at which point clear advice about staying legal must be offered, and some sites may need to be screened out. However, the concept of inclusion must permit any adult in care to pursue legal sexual interests on the Internet when in the privacy of their own home.

How IT Works

Motivation

RICHARD

The key to getting people with learning disabilities to use computers is to find something which really interests them and use the computer as a tool to build on that interest. Richard wanted to attend computer sessions but it was difficult for the tutor to get him involved even in one-to-one sessions. Richard has no verbal communication and he will not leave his house to participate in community activities. He has no hobbies and doesn't like many television programmes and rarely has visits from his family.

So how could the tutor who knows little of Richard's background engage him when using the computer? The tutor used some lateral thinking! Richard takes pride in the way he dresses and loves to collect unusual T-shirts. On his first visit to Richard's house the tutor remarked on Richard's T-shirt and realised from his response how pleased Richard was. So when the session began the tutor decided to use the T-shirt to engage Richard. They talked about the colour, the picture on the T-shirt and where Richard had bought the T-shirt. Then the tutor wrote down the description for Richard to copy in MS Word.

On the next few occasions when they met Richard wore a different T-shirt and immediately pointed to the picture. On one occasion Richard wore a T-shirt which a friend had bought on holiday in Australia. The tutor used the opportunity to look on the Internet with Richard and find out more information on Australia. Gradually, Richard was moved away from the T-shirts and learned new IT skills and enjoyed his sessions. He likes to copy-type so the tutor moved Richard on to using Writing With Symbols (Widgit Software Ltd) and created a list of names (for example animals) for which he knows there are symbols. Richard has learned that if a symbol does not appear when he has typed a word then he has mis-typed it and will self-correct the word.

Emotional support

MICHAEL

For many people with learning disabilities, showing their emotions and dealing with grief are difficult processes. Michael is 58 and has lived in the same residential home for 40 years. He is quite able and has a part-time job in the post room of a large bank and is able to catch the bus on his own. Michael's mother died several years ago and Michael never mentions her nor will he be drawn into any form of conversation about her, even to his brother whom he sees often.

Michael has chosen not to attend computer sessions in his local day-services but he has shown an interest in other people's sessions, keeping a watchful eye on progress from the back of the room. When Princess Diana died Michael wanted to go to the funeral, when it was explained to him that this was not appropriate, he was really disappointed. It was suggested that he could sign the condolence book on the Internet. He was supported to do this and he thought long and hard about what he would write in the book. Following this he said he would like to write a letter to the young princes as he could remember what it felt like when his own mother died. Michael was supported to write a letter and he expressed his own grief and started talking about his mum. For Michael the icing on the cake was when he received a letter from Buckingham Palace thanking him for his best wishes.

Michael is now a regular user of the computer. He uses the Internet to follow royal events and look at the royal websites. He also writes regular letters to his brother and has written a short story about his mother.

ROBERT

Robert is in his early 40s and lives in a small residential house with five others. He is quite articulate but does not enjoy being in large crowds, preferring to stay in the house rather than attend day-services or local college. Robert has one older brother who rarely visits and Robert has never been invited to his brother's house. He has no other family members.

Robert's mother died some time ago, after a long illness. Robert visited her in hospital just before her death but was not invited to (nor told about) her funeral. Wanting to support Robert through his grief and to allow him to say a proper goodbye to his mother, his support worker, Leah, worked with Robert. They decided that they would have a memorial ceremony and plant a tree in the garden of Robert's house in remembrance of his mother. Leah supported Robert to help him to decide what he would like written on the plaque beside the tree. Then they wrote a short speech together using symbols to support the text (Writing With Symbols from Widgit Software Ltd) so that he could read this at the ceremony. Then Robert made the invitations to his guests (people he lives with and staff) using Microsoft Publisher and wrote a shopping list for refreshments.

Robert was very proud of his invitations and the speech which he had written on the computer. He was able to take digital photos of the tree planting and of the ceremony and he has these on his computer as a constant reminder, together with the one photo he has of his mother, to refer to whenever he feels the need. These have also been printed out in a book so that he can keep them in his own room.

Workskills: working as a team

As well as learning new skills for work it is important to know how to work with other people. In one day-service they decided that team working is really important and so they set up a newsletter group. Each member of the team was given their own specific job as well as being part of the editorial team. The group is made up of four people whose roles are gathering recipes and jokes, interviewing a member of staff (or someone else), taking photographs and designing the front cover.

They each take their role very seriously and the 'interviewer' decides who should be interviewed for the current edition and then writes a list of questions she will ask. She has a few standard questions which she asks each person being interviewed, but always tries to include new questions. She types these out on the computer before the interview. When all of the material has been gathered together the group meet to decide how the newsletter should be laid out and then they work together to produce the final edition (with full support from staff).

The team are so proud of their newsletter that the distribution list which started only as a few people in the day-service has expanded to include parents and families and others within their organisation. Their computer skills have increased and they use the Internet to research some of their articles, always looking for new recipes and interesting features. Recently one of the team came across an online newsletter and pointed it out to the others. They are now exploring the possibility of publishing their newsletter on the web.

Inclusion: email group

For people who find integrating into the community difficult because of their disabilities (be they learning, physical or communication disabilities) the Internet, and particularly email, can be very empowering. When receiving an email it is impossible to create a stereotype of the sender. A group of people with learning and physical disabilities from a day-service in Kingston, London were encouraged to form an email group. They learned the skills of sending and receiving emails initially by sending them to family members and to each other.

Having grasped the concept of emails the group decided to email further afield and as one of the group was an avid listener of a local radio station they decided to send an email to a favourite presenter. They all discussed the content of the email and what they wanted to say about themselves and what their interests are. They sent the email and were delighted when they received a reply. However, their excitement increased when they read the email and discovered that they had all been invited to visit the radio station for a guided tour. The visit was brilliant and there is now regular contact between the radio station staff and the email group.

Having been encouraged by this response another member of the group wanted to email a local football team. This they did and were delighted to, once again, be invited to visit the football ground for a tour. Their appetite has now been well and truly whetted and they are emailing celebrities in the hope of meeting them – or at the very least getting autographs for their growing collection!

Independence

RICKY

Ricky is a 35-year-old man who lives in a small residential home in a market town in the Cotswolds. He attends a local day centre and enjoys all forms of art and craft and using the computer. One of the staff, Wendy, has some really imaginative ideas for projects for the eight people who regularly attend the day-service. One day Ricky asked Wendy why he couldn't read like she could. Wendy set out to teach Ricky to read using Rebus symbols from Writing With Symbols (Widgit Software Ltd).

Wendy typed a few short sentences using the computer programme, printed these out and made a book for Ricky. She then made 'flash cards' using the same symbols so that Ricky could match them to the sentences in his book. The first sentences contained only three words such as 'I like chips' – all words which have easily learned/recognisable symbols. By changing the noun at the end of the sentence Ricky was able to create new sentences by just changing one symbol. Once he had learned a few symbols Wendy would arrange the flash cards into sentences so that Ricky could read them. Once he had learned the verb 'like' Wendy introduced a new verb 'can' and some new nouns. Gradually new words/symbols were introduced such as 'and' so that sentences could be made longer.

Ricky wanted to show his reading skills to a visitor to the day-service. He went and retrieved his special box of flash cards and Wendy arranged a short sentence which Ricky read with glee. Then Wendy said she would make a long sentence so that he could really show off his skills. In order to give Ricky time to work out the sentence before he read it aloud she started talking to the visitor. However, Ricky butted in to tell Wendy she had made a mistake by missing out a word and that the sentence didn't make sense. He was right!

Case studies

SARAH

Sarah, aged 42, lives in a residential home which she shares with two others. They have a computer in the communal area which is connected to the Internet. Sarah had shown an interest in using computers to access her favourite 'soap' stars on the Internet. She began to collect information about them and someone suggested that she collect the same sort of information about herself for other people to see. Sarah was excited at creating her own lifestory and asked her parents to send photographs from her childhood and of other family members. Her parents were very supportive and not only sent photos but a written summarised lifestory with key dates and events.

Sarah worked with one staff member to create a multimedia lifestory. They began by discussing how the lifestory would be organised. Sarah had very strong ideas of what she wanted in it and brought with her 152 photos – all of which she wanted to be included! Sarah also brought in some of her paintings which she had done when on holiday with her parents. None of the staff who worked with her knew that she could paint so well and for some this made them see Sarah in a new positive light.

Once the lifestory was completed (at least the first 40 years) Sarah was asked to show some extracts and talk about it at a national ICT conference. She was able to show people all the things that ordinarily she would not have mentioned – things like her visit to the *Neighbours* film set when on holiday to Australia. This was a very empowering process for her and she has since shown her lifestory, and talked about what it means to her, to staff attending lifestory workshops. Sarah also asked for many copies of the lifestory which she then sent to family and friends worldwide. She received many emails in response and this established new links through email with family who had not previously been able to communicate with Sarah. She now regularly receives emails (short text) with current photos which she keeps to add to her ongoing lifestory.

JULIAN

Julian has lived in residential care for more than 25 years. He has very little verbal communication and high support needs. Recently Julian went to visit his mother who was in her 90s. She handed her precious family photos to Julian's support worker as he wanted to start Julian's lifestory. She was able to give a great deal of background information about the photos, information which otherwise would have been lost as she died only weeks after this visit. Julian's mother described how difficult it had been for his professional father to accept Julian and revealed some details which explain Julian's behaviour now.

Julian loved looking at the photos of his childhood and was able to communicate in his own way some of his memories. Producing his lifestory with Julian was a slow and difficult process, not at all similar to the lifestory produced with Sarah who is very articulate and able to describe events and memories. Julian's support worker took short video clips which were used in his lifestory to replace text.

For the first time in many years Julian attended his care review meeting as he wanted to show everyone his lifestory. He was able to press the right buttons on the computer (having been involved in the lifestory-producing process from the beginning) and it was obvious from his delight when the videos played and he saw photos of people he recognised that he had been part of the process. Everyone was surprised that Julian had participated meaningfully in the meeting but none more than his brother, who was close to tears as he said that he was, for the first time, proud of his brother!

LIFESTORY OF A HOUSE!

The six tenants of a house in Devon all have autism, none have verbal communication and all have high support needs. This has meant a large staff team and a huge turnover in staffing. When new staff visit the house for the first time the tenants are not able to give them a guided tour in the normal way and so it is left to someone else (invariably another member of staff) to show them around their home.

One of the staff members, Liz, decided that if the tenants were unable to physically give a guided tour then they could do it virtually. Having already completed a couple of lifestories Liz decided to work with the group and complete a 'lifestory' of the house. The front page is a photograph of the front of the house, recognisable to all the tenants. By clicking on the front door the user moves onto the next page which is a photo of the hallway and all the doors leading off it. Clicking on each door takes the user into another room – conservatory, kitchen, lounge, dining room. If the user clicks on the stairs they are shown the top of the stairs and all the doors there. Each door has a photo of the room's occupant and clicking on the door takes the user into a mini lifestory of the person who lives there. Similarly clicking on the kitchen door shows the staff team and clicking on each photo gives a short biography of that person.

The group enjoyed working on the house's lifestory and helping to take photos and choose the photos which would be included. They have a computer with a touch monitor and when a new person visits the house they are able to be in control of the first tour of the house and to join in with the information being given about them and their home.

DANIEL

Daniel is in his mid-30s and has lived in a small residential home with five other people who, like Daniel, need high levels of support. Daniel is unable to communicate verbally but he has a good sense of humour and likes to share his jokes with everyone. As part of his person-centred plan Daniel worked with his support worker, Mike, to complete his multimedia lifestory. This included a timetable for a normal week in Daniel's life.

When they got to Tuesday afternoon the support worker said that Daniel has a 'free' afternoon when he likes to watch videos. An onlooker asked what his favourite videos were and Daniel hummed the theme tune to James Bond. All of the audio material for the lifestory had, to this point, been recorded by Mike, but now he took the opportunity to include Daniel in this process and recorded him humming the James Bond theme tune. When this was played back to Daniel he was delighted. This was the first time he had ever had his voice recorded and he insisted on everyone in the house listening to it!

When they came to add photos for the 'lunch' part of the timetable Mike said that everyone in the house had sandwiches for lunch but Daniel doesn't like sandwiches so he has baked beans on toast which are his absolute favourite and he has them every day! Mike went on to the Internet to find photos of 'beans on toast'. When he imported one into Daniel's timetable Daniel reacted very positively and let Mike know in no uncertain terms that he did *not* want beans every day. Through working with Daniel on his lifestory staff have learned new things about Daniel and his daily routine has changed because of this – a truly person-centred approach!

Chapter 2

Beginning to Take Control

As discussed in the Introduction, government thinking about personal autonomy is laudable, as expressed, for example, in the concepts of person-centred planning set out in Valuing People (Department of Health 2001), and elsewhere. Making the reality live up to the ideal is another matter. To some people receiving care – and to some people providing care – the gap between what is written down and the world they actually inhabit may seem too huge to cross. Carers are supposed to use the person-centred planning process to ensure that the people for whom they care have 'rights, independence, choice and inclusion'. The first challenge to overcome in doing this is the bald fact that people on the receiving end of paid care are dependent on that care in many areas of their lives. Where disabilities are purely physical the areas of dependence are clear-cut: these people can still make their views known and their individual autonomy need not otherwise be compromised. When a person's disabilities entail cognitive and communicative difficulties dependencies of another kind are created.

Those we are caring for to whom this applies depend on us to make their communications effective and to maximise their understanding of the confusing universe. Carers need to notice, process, understand and respond. As individuals who know other individuals well, we may be very tuned in and quick to understand those we care about. But when it comes to fostering independence, this close attention and rich contextualised interpretation can be counterproductive: it tends to put the carer in the middle of the communication loop, an essential connection if effective transmission is to occur. Thus we may easily compound dependency with too much love. On the other hand, if we do not play this role how do those for whom we care speak out? We need to help them to speak out for themselves, not take them over. Yet we also need to communicate our own knowledge and understanding as clearly and effectively as possible so that it helps us make sense of the confusing world. Communication is a two-way process and is not just about carers 'doing the understanding'.

As far as possible, we need to step back while making sure an alternative communicative tool is in place which is meaningful and accessible both to the individual and to other people. If we don't make sure this happens, the person's voice will remain unheard and the person-centred planning process will be a sham.

Our heroes[1]

Marie has lost her short-term memory. She is a 72-year-old widow with scattered children and grandchildren. She was a secretary for much of her life before and after having children, but retired early to look after her older husband. Since her husband died she has lived with her sister, who has now died herself. Marie remembers the distant past very well but sometimes confuses her grandchildren with her own children. Marie now lives in a care home where she has her own room, phone and furniture, but she has had to give her cat away. She still knits enthusiastically and has a treasure trove of knitting patterns. Marie has always sent cards to all her grandchildren and has their birth dates in a special book, but she does not see them much in person. She has never personally used a computer.

Kumar is 22 years old. He is an only son with two younger sisters. His full name, Ratna Kumar, meaning 'gem', got him called 'Ratty' at school so he prefers to use just his surname. He has a diagnosis of Asperger syndrome and was at mainstream school until the age of 16 when he left because of bullying by fellow pupils, and by teachers convinced that his obvious intelligence meant he could 'shape up' if he chose to (for example they insisted Kumar use hand-writing rather than a keyboard for all written work). Kumar's move to special school made him much happier, and in many ways he flourished there as an exceptionally able young person, although he did not get any A-levels. His mother was happy because he was happy, but his father was ashamed to see his only son labelled dysfunctional. Now that Kumar's sisters are teenagers, their older brother's lack of social skills and occasional outbursts have become a source of embarrassment, even though his youngest sister, Nita, is greatly attached to him. So Kumar now lives in his own flat, bought by his parents, using direct payments to pay for the support he needs. He's lucky that in his local authority it's recognised that having a high IQ does not necessarily guarantee basic life skills. Kumar owns his own computer and has been using it since early childhood, but has not, until recently, been allowed to use the Internet.

1   We call them 'our heroes' partly to reflect their role at the centre of this book, partly because each of them has and will overcome many and grave difficulties during the course of their lives.

Irene comes from a large family which moved to London when she was a toddler, in 1949. By the time she was three Irene stood out from the rest of the family as strikingly unmanageable. Playschool couldn't cope, and school said she was unteachable. At the age of nine Irene was moved permanently to a longstay hospital while her other many siblings stayed at home. Eventually Irene lost touch with them all and it's said that the parents broke up. She was discharged 'into the community' in the mid-1990s after four decades in the institution. At that point she was given a label of 'moderate to severe learning disability with autistic tendencies'. Along with half a dozen other people from the hospital Irene now lives in a comfortable suburban house with a middle-sized garden; like everyone else, she has a room to herself.

Irene is not obviously tuned in to speech – but she does occasionally reveal some understanding. She very rarely speaks, but sometimes shouts loud and long. The only things which seem to really amuse Irene are breakages, although she takes no steps to make them happen, if someone breaks a glass or a piece of crockery she will laugh till she cries. She will enter or leave a room in response to music of various sorts. Irene goes to the nearby day centre on some days but does not join in any activities. Staff tend to regard the idea of doing person-centred planning with Irene as anything from absurd to impossible. Staff sometimes need reminding that Irene has many, many reasons for being so angry, and that 'challenging behaviours' are not necessarily evidence of psychiatric abnormality. Irene has only glimpsed the computer in the staff office, and no-one so far has thought of introducing her to a computer with the idea of her using it.

We'll now take a look at what support these three very different people need in the very basic areas we identified in Chapter 1 (developed from the Law Society's thoughts on the topic via the government's capacity legislation) and at how best to provide that support. As the book progresses we will see how these apply in particular instances; for now, here is a general overview.

Identifying and accessing relevant information

Even if you have unimpaired capacity, you may have difficulty both in working out what would be relevant for you to find out, and in actually finding it out. All three of our characters would have difficulty in picking up a phone, phoning a relevant person, and making appropriate inquiries. All three of them would have difficulty in going to a library and accessing the information services there. All three would be unlikely even to identify their own information needs beyond their most immediately pressing interests. All three are likely to be unaware of possibilities which strike other people as obvious. Unfortunately, they are also liable to confusion and information overload, so very great care must be taken in adjusting to and supporting their information needs.

Understanding information relevant to the decision

Information must be presented in a way which minimises confusion and overload: it must be adjusted to individual levels of understanding, it must be clear, literal and avoid ambiguity, and it must be simple without oversimplification (for discussion see Thurman, Jones and Tarleton 2005). Equally important, it must be seen as relevant: people need to understand not just the information itself but the point of learning that information. Taking new unsought information on board tends not to be effortless, and it takes time. The people we are discussing will not make the effort or take the time if they cannot see the point. Support in this area must include helping individuals understand why this or that decision matters to them, and thus how their own interests are affected by the information in question.

Much more time than is usually allowed in conversation may be needed for processing speech or signing. This is one of the ways in which writing and other recorded symbol systems have the advantage: they can give you as much time as you need. You can also break them up into your own manageable chunks if that suits you. Another important benefit is that recorded symbols have no additional intonation meaning or body language to process. And of course it is easy to revisit anything written down as often as you wish and thus increase your chances of understanding it fully. People sometimes talk of presenting information 'visually' as the key to improving intelligibility. But we suspect the advantage of visual material is that it confers permanence and the potential for indefinitely frequent 'meaning-refreshment' as much as its distinctive sensory modality. In principle recorded and replayable audio material could be just as useful, and might be preferred by some people. However, many, though not all, autistic people express a preference for taking information in through vision rather than hearing, and are likely to strongly prefer the written to the spoken word.

Of our three characters, Kumar is the most capable of achieving a full understanding of new information in itself. However, he may also miss much of what seems obvious to other people, and as a result has built some of his belief system on very shaky foundations. Supporting his information needs will include ensuring that new information is anchored in sound basic relevant beliefs. It may also be particularly hard to get Kumar to appreciate the value of information which he is not aware of missing, or to focus his attention outside his current interests. All new information offered to Kumar should be connected to those interests or it will not be recognised by him as relevant and it will not be absorbed. Once he has realised the relevance of some new information he may have problems in becoming certain about that information; its newness and the lack of his own personal validation of it may keep worrying him and prompt him to ask repeated questions.

Marie still has perfect linguistic knowledge and will basically understand the meaning of what is said to her. Marie also, unlike either Kumar or Irene, has a good basic understanding of how the world works. However, she is likely to understand what is said much better if everyone and everything referred to has been familiar to her for years. New people, places, things or ideas must be introduced with care, explained, and preferably illustrated. This often needs to be done repeatedly, thus underlining once more the case for having the information recorded in some form, and accessible as needed. Ensuring that happens may spare much of the strain on staff who are attempting to support the information needs of people like Kumar and Marie.

Irene's case is different again. It can be extremely hard to tell what, if anything, Irene has understood, and apart from food, breakages and music, it is not obvious that she has any particular interests. Even so, everyone concerned thinks that Irene is noticing what goes on around her, and forming opinions of it – perhaps usually hostile opinions. Since she has had control over almost nothing in her life since entering the institution more than 40 years ago, Irene has no expectations of being able to make choices about matters which concern her. So that may be the first thing she needs to understand, i.e. that there is a real potential for her to take effective constructive action. In practice Irene's sources of information are invariably drawn from personal experience, which of course restricts the range of information she can access.

Retaining information relevant to the decision

An extreme difference between our three protagonists appears in relation to the issue of information retention. When Kumar has learned something it is usually learned exceptionally thoroughly – if he is interested he will learn exhaustively and permanently from all available sources of information; if he is not interested he will not learn at all. Irene may learn what she does learn equally permanently and thoroughly. It is very hard to tell how much she actually knows or understands, but what she knows is confined to and derived from her immediate experience and affects her future behaviour. While Kumar may remember word for word what someone has said to him (without necessarily understanding it), there is no evidence whatever that Irene ever remembers what is said to her. She appears never to learn by being told. But if she is, for example, shown a place and given the opportunity to explore it, then on the next visit she will know her way around.

For both Irene and Kumar, just as for most people, finding things out because they are interested is what works for them, i.e. this is the information they will both seek and retain. Sadly, this is no longer true of Marie except in respect of knitting patterns, which she can still follow well. So long as you can keep track of where you are in a knitting pattern, one line at a time is all you need retain. She has long used a sliding rule which fits over a knitting pattern to put a window round the line she's working on. In other matters Marie is no longer capable of taking in new information easily. Even when she understands some information perfectly clearly, she does not retain it. But Marie does know what she wants in the way of food, comfort and company, and she retains the will and the ability to communicate those wants. What Marie needs is a medium outside herself in which to retain the information she can't retain in her mind any longer, indeed she often writes lists (but also tends to lose them).

Using that relevant information as part of the process of making the decision

In a simple case such as, say, choosing what to eat, the relevant information will just be whatever the options are. You can't decide what to have for supper without using the relevant knowledge that there is, for example, shepherd's pie or spaghetti bolognaise for supper. But in more complex decision-making processes (perhaps with much more far-reaching consequences), what information is relevant, and how it is relevant, will almost always be less obvious. But then, as we have seen, identifying and understanding relevant information depends on having interests which are affected by it. It should follow that if the earlier stages of this process, described above, have been satisfactory, the relevant information will automatically be informing the decision-making process. In other words if you have identified and accessed relevant information because you have appreciated its relevance, that information will *ipso facto* affect the current state of the interest which is being pursued.

However, in complicated situations it is easy to wind up, however able you are, with only a partial understanding of the implications of new information. For example, you might learn that in order to attend a college course you have to be 'approved' for it, but you might not understand that to get that approval you are going to have to be on your best behaviour every day for weeks. You might not even understand how or why other people judge you as behaving well, or not. So your decisions about how to behave on any given day may not be affected by that general requirement. This brings us back to the initial problems of identifying and accessing relevant information in the first place, of understanding what its relevance is, and retaining it when it is useful.

Everybody benefits from other people's help in resolving such issues and in recognising what may be possible. Our protagonists probably need a bit more help than most people, but there's no fundamental difference. There is, however, a practical difference of great significance, i.e. the facility for communicating their own needs. Although Kumar has a great vocabulary he does not appear to realise that the people around him do not know what he wants. Irene seems to assume nobody knows or cares what she wants, and has no active speech to tell it anyway. For these different reasons both Kumar and Irene have problems in understanding the point of communication, but Marie does not. Marie loves communication for itself and always has.

Communicating that decision (whether by talking, using sign language or any other means)

Every communicative act must connect an output, an expression of some kind, with an input, a witness of that expression. If it is a successful communication, then the person who has seen or heard it will understand the expression as meaningful *and* understand its specific meaning. If it is a successful social act, it will evoke a response which constructively addresses that meaning and supports a shared positive emotional state.

Kumar has no difficulty engaging in communication which other people understand as meaningful. He makes himself understood using his excellent mastery of grammar and vocabulary, which strikes some people as an absurdly pedantic and longwinded style of speech, though they usually do understand what he is saying. Kumar does not adjust his speech style or his topics to suit his listeners. He sometimes provokes mockery from the uncouth, and he often 'loses his audience'. That means that from Kumar's perspective, most other people rarely constructively address his concerns. Far from bolstering his spirits Kumar's attempts at communicating are often responded to in ways that make him feel much worse. This is especially true among those who do not know him well. Luckily his mother and his sister Nita make encouraging exceptions to this pattern, but Kumar is beginning to feel his social isolation.

Kumar frequently does not grasp specific meaning in what other people are saying to him because what they say so often has pronouns in it, goes beyond the literal meaning of the words uttered, and has extra meaning in its intonation and the speaker's body language. Because Kumar is not tuned in to other people's interests he is often baffled by the incomplete and allusive things they say. So he tends neither to give nor to receive the constructive tuned-in feedback which from either party could turn the communication into a successful social event. In addition, Kumar needs other people to adjust their emotional states to his emotional state. He has not yet acquired any awareness of other people's distinct internal lives, and has no facility for adjusting his emotional states to theirs. Kumar has the potential to be an excellent communicator, but he is becoming so frustrated at the way it keeps going wrong that he is trying less and less often to communicate with anyone outside his family. This compounds his exclusion from all but the narrowest of communities.

So, even if Kumar eventually sees the point of telling other people his hopes and fears, he may still lack the motivation and confidence to do so. Furthermore, outside his immediate family, he is likely to have problems discriminating between people to whom it is appropriate to disclose personal information and those to whom it is not, and he may not know how to identify and access the key people who can affect the outcomes he seeks.

Irene rarely gets past the first communicative hurdle of having the meaningful expressions she produces recognised as such. If they are recognised as having a meaning it still does not follow that their specific meaning will be identified, often people just know she is upset about something and they have no idea what. Irene herself rarely gives evidence that she recognises other people's attempts at communication as meaningful, and still less often that she understands what they mean. Other people do not accommodate to Irene's meanings, and she does not accommodate to theirs. She has hardly ever enjoyed the happy business of exchanging meanings and sharing positive emotional states. Indeed, Irene is seen as having unpredictable outbursts or tantrums which other people find 'challenging', i.e. other people keenly wish she would stop behaving like that. From the point of view of other people, constructive engagement with Irene often means getting her to stop rampaging around hitting herself and making frightening noises. A positive emotional mood tends to be a long time coming for everyone after these communicative exchanges. She needs other people to back off, be patient, sensitive and not think the worst of her.

The situation for Marie is very different at the moment. She has always had high levels of social skills, and in many ways she retains those and charms the people around her. Her main problem with other people's meanings is her repeated puzzlement with references to anything only encountered by her in recent months: she has almost completely ceased to take anything new on board. This means, for example, that although Marie asks polite questions of her carers such as, 'How is your husband these days?' she does not take the answer in, but continues to remember that it is a good question to ask so will ask it again and again of the same person. She also needs repeated reminders of where things are. When this part of the communication equation is missing, that is, when the adaptive response of retaining new information doesn't happen and old information seems new over and over again, other people tend to find it anything from laughable to deeply irritating. It can have a profound effect on their attitudes; they are likely to make Marie feel scorned and derided unless they are very careful.

Functioning within a calm and supportive emotional climate

Sometimes maintaining calm and being supportive can seem an impossible challenge for carers. As we have seen, good communication typically results in a positive shared emotional state, but this is a process which tends to go wrong in various ways for our three protagonists. Instead of communication resulting in happy unison for them and their carers, communication tends to lead to a worsening of the emotional climate. Just being talked at can wind up both Irene and Kumar and make them feel they are being hassled. Angry, anxious or disgruntled people are probably at their least receptive, their least creative and their most likely to screw up. People need time free of emotional pressure if they are to make good decisions. If emotional temperature heats up and tension rises, the best way to reduce the stress is almost always to allow maximum space and time.

Among the great things about communicating through writing is the fact that it doesn't impose instant rapid processing of transient signals as speech does. It does not demand an immediate response and does not have additional parallel emotional character as speech does. While the writing of personal letters has seen a rapid decline, the writing of personal emails has become part of ordinary life. Computer use has the added benefit of involving interaction with an object without emotions or body language of its own, which can be switched off and left alone – or even abused – without offence. The main hazard in the use of computers in care homes could be staff who are themselves so anxious around computers that they inject their own tension into the situation.

> They just assume that everybody has computers, as though we who don't are second class citizens. (BBC Radio 4 phone-in, March 2005)

Using IT

You might think that specialised software would be essential for getting people with learning disabilities to engage with computers. A huge amount of such software has been written especially for school use, and can be very helpful especially where there are specific educational goals. However, with few exceptions, by their very nature special programmes emphasise the difference and relative disability of those who use them. They can therefore have an excluding rather than including effect, at least in the short term. Evident mastery of software which is in general use is perhaps more likely to stimulate respect from other people than is mastery of specially adapted software. Symbol-to/from-text translation software (discussed below) is one of the partial exceptions to that. Another significant exception is the software which has been developed by SEMERC (Special Education Micro-Electronics Resource Centre) with the Home Farm Trust to help prepare people for action in the real world. This lifeskills software called *Out and About 1: The Living Community* and *Out and About 2: Around the Home* is among the first lifeskills software produced for older learners and is therefore age-appropriate for adults. Although young Kumar is the character in this book who is most familiar with computers and probably has the highest measurable 'IQ', he is also the one who will benefit most from exploring this *Out and About* software. He may learn things about ordinary life from it which will help prevent him from producing the sort of social gaffe that so often spirals into catastrophe for him and deepens his social exclusion. Indeed, one of the activities in *Out and About 1* promotes discussion between the user and tutor/staff about appropriate behaviour in a variety of settings including the supermarket, restaurant, bank and college through the use of video clips.

In general the absolutely mainstream programme PowerPoint will be our main tool for storing and presenting information in accessible form. PowerPoint was developed as a way of allowing senior executives who knew nothing about computers to use their amazing, trendy laptops to present company data with impressive aplomb. According to one article, 'there are tracts of corporate America where to appear without PowerPoint would be vaguely pretentious, like wearing no shoes' (Parker 2001). PowerPoint is extraordinarily simple to use, and its capacity to handle material of every sort with virtuoso animated graphics is stunning ('all singing all dancing' is a doddle, if often a mistake).

The Internet is the other major tool for empowerment and inclusion which will empower our heroes. One extraordinary power the Internet confers is that of communicating with people of every sort in every place in the world. One of the areas in which specialist software can come into its own is in enabling translation into text of messages written by people who are using symbol systems such as Makaton or Widgit (see Inter_Comm, a symbolised email programme from Widgit.com, and also Communicate: Webwide, also from Widgit.com). This type of communicative tool can do a great job in reducing the gap between people who write or understand text and people who don't. For example, it can enable an exchange of emails which 'cuts out the middle man' for someone with expertise in symbolic but not alphabetical written systems. That said, the authors of this book believe that every possible encouragement should be given to people to learn their culture's written forms. For some people the use of symbols/graphics helpfully supports the text and gives them some 'clue' as to the meaning – these people may even be taught to 'read' symbols even when they never learn to read text. However, it should be noted that there is a great deal of evidence, anecdotal and otherwise, that many non-speaking people on the autism spectrum can read and may be capable of using a keyboard to write (see, e.g. www.gettingthetruthout.org). That may also be true for other people with learning disabilities and communication problems.

The Internet also provides the most powerful and effective way of finding specific information. The power to find out almost anything one wants to know is made possible by Google, the search engine which trawls the whole Internet in a flash for the data you seek. The number of people who use Google is growing so rapidly that by the time you read this book it may even be true that most people use Google. Certainly the authors of this book would feel as though they had lost an eye or a hand if they lost their access to Google. As well as giving you a way to find answers to all your questions, Google will be one of the best ways of finding material to put into your PowerPoint shows. The main function of scanners and cameras will be to do the same. Google is expanding all the time and the authors are enjoying the new additions of Google Answers and Google Maps (see the 'more»' section of the Google.com website).

As it happens, not only are two out of three of our heroes in the 'least likely to use a computer' and 'least likely to use the Internet' sections of the population, so are the vast majority of those who care for them. Many people reading this book may be doing so nervously, reluctantly, and because they know they are supposed to learn about this stuff. Marie has just the same anxious and slightly defiant attitude to using information technology in the shape of computers as most of her carers do. Irene has no attitude to information technology so far, apart from her general reluctance to engage in anything actively suggested to her. Kumar, though expert in some areas of computer use, has not had access to the Internet until now, and tends mainly to use his computer for playing games.

Before we can get IT in use to help the decision-making processes of these people, we have to get them to make and express the initial decision to investigate some information technology which is accessible to them. Once again, as with any learning process, the key is motivation – if people can see a reason to try something new then maybe they will. If they can see no reason to try something new then we can be sure they will not. We have to get them interested. Because there is an IT angle on just about everything (all right, not smells so far, and they have not made much headway with texture) this may be easier than it sounds.

A good place to start might be to do an informal audit of technology used by carers in order to assess the range of ways they communicate with the help of information technology. Carers may be surprised at how much they already know and do with information technology compared with the people who use carers' services. For example, in one report all the staff at one day centre used mobile phones and none of the centre users did; many of the staff used email, none of the centre users did.

Mobile phones are really just small portable objects through which connections with all manner of other technologies as well as people can be made. They are becoming less and less like phones and more and more like multimedia ports through which sounds, images (still or moving) and texts can all flow or be stored. More recent models can be linked to a computer and even directly to the Internet, so that pictures which you take with your phone or recordings you make with it can be winging round the world in a flash, or be stored for posterity on the Internet. More modestly, if you know how to read then you can use even the quaintest mobile phone to keep in touch with, for example, your grandchildren, cheaply and easily through text messaging.

When Marie moved from home her daughter made sure phone calls would be diverted to a new mobile phone. It is an up-to-the-minute nifty little thing with a fold-out screen and the capacity to take and show photos of reasonable quality and poorer quality videos. Marie has so far never used it as anything but a telephone, but the right sort of encouragement might easily launch her into more adventurous use of her mobile. For example, showing her someone else's similar phone taking and receiving pictures might do the trick, or getting one of her grandchildren to send her a picture, or vice versa is likely to be enticing. Marie wants to keep in touch with all her children and grandchildren, and see pictures of them as they grow up, so this is likely to be highly motivating for her.

Kumar doesn't go out very much and does not make phone calls either. He does get phoned sometimes by his sister Nita, and by his mother every day. When Kumar is given a mobile phone like Marie's, his first use of it is to take photographs of every room in his flat and put them on his computer. So far Kumar has not been moved to use the phone in any other way except to answer it if it rings. But he likes it very much as an object and will agree to take it with him when he goes out – this makes it much less worrying all round if Kumar goes out on his own. How to use the phone's memory has been rehearsed with him. As well as his mother's and sister's numbers being programmed in to the phone, so are his own home number and that of Rob, his key worker.

Irene has never used a phone of any sort – but shows some shy interest when shown someone's mobile with a text message of her name on its little screen. Perhaps one day Irene might learn to use a texting phone or other keyboard in the same way: many people who do not talk do read and can happily take advantage of the perfectly formed letters of a keyboard.

The possibilities of using keyboards to encourage expression in people who did not speak first attracted attention in the context of a practice known as 'facilitated communication' (FC). First developed to help people with cerebral palsy control their tremor enough to strike keys on a keyboard accurately, FC involved laying a hand lightly on the arm. Its use spread to the world of autism and learning disabilities, and was at first hailed with enthusiasm. However, after a while it became clear that in many cases the 'facilitators' were more in control than the individuals whom they were supposed to be helping, and the reputation of this approach became badly tarnished. Even so, there has been plentiful anecdotal evidence of individual successes over the years, and many families are convinced that their learning disabled member has genuinely used a keyboard with a facilitator's help. Only recently has some indisputable evidence emerged that in at least some cases the individuals using keyboards in cases of FC are indeed in control (Grayson 2004). The people in his study are all non-speaking adults with autistic tendencies, and they are all able to produce clear and articulate sentences using this method.

Sadly, unless the facilitator is faded out fairly early on in the learning experience the people using the keyboard are likely to develop a dependency on having a facilitator's encouraging touch, or worse still a dependency on a particular individual. But it is clear from Grayson's work that we cannot ever dismiss the possibility that someone is literate and potentially articulate just because they do not speak (see also www.autistics.org/library). Therefore, it is of key importance in facilitated communication that the support is faded out as rapidly as seems feasible in order to encourage independence.

Irene might need some guided hands-on experience before she realises that pressing the keys will produce a letter on the screen, probably best done using a full-size computer keyboard. If Irene can be persuaded to the computer-face, she may need to watch someone else in action on it many times, and she may need to be repeatedly offered the chance of trying the keyboard without super-vision before she will venture to do so. If she is showing a real interest in the computer and if someone gets on well enough with Irene to take her hand and show her how hitting the keys with a finger produces perfect symbols on the screen, that just might speed up the process. Any help of this sort must of course be offered sensitively as well as being sensitively faded out.

So, why would Irene pay any attention to a computer? What might have the effect of drawing her towards that alien screen? Perhaps having her name writ large on the monitor would be of interest to her, but would she notice it? She is not likely to take a look because somebody suggests she should, rather the opposite. This could be where the multimedia aspects of today's computers come into their own. We know Irene is drawn to some sorts of music, and that she finds events like plates and glasses being smashed very compelling. One way of attracting her to the machine would be to choose some music she is known to like and use the computer to play it. But that might result in Irene seeing the computer as just another music machine and of no special interest. Playing the music using something like Windows Media player which has a facility to project moving images which move in time with the music could take her interest a stage further. Or it could be incorporated into a PowerPoint show (Helpsheets A and B). But even if Irene did become interested in the multimedia effects, would this motivate her to use the keyboard? Those programmes can be interacted with and different effects chosen by pressing the right button – some people might find that so intriguing that they want to keep pressing the button and exploring the possibilities, but from what we know of Irene that, at the moment, it is unlikely in her case.

Instead of using music to lure Irene to the multimedia potential of the computer, the siren call of breaking glass could be tried instead. Breaking glass has a very distinctive sound, and recordings of it can easily be found on the Internet – or easily made and stored digitally, as we shall see. A staged approach to exploiting these possibilities would probably work best. First get the breaking glass sounds playing automatically at regular intervals – you can make a PowerPoint show do this in which each sound is accompanied by a matching image (see next chapter). Then switch off the autopilot and show Irene how you can initiate a new image and matching sound by hitting the space bar, or the enter key, or an up/down arrow button. This could be done both by showing by example and, if appropriate, by showing with hand over hand so that Irene gets the feel of what's happening. It is not hard to find images of breaking glass or crockery on the Internet, so each different sound could have a different image. This is almost certain to attract and amuse Irene, and to hold her interest for longer than anything else at this initial stage. So, now that she is interested and expecting things to happen, Irene can be shown how to make them happen herself, with one simple movement in this extremely user-friendly programme. This can be repeated as often as it takes. Carers need to show how, indicate that it is fine for Irene to do it too, any time – and then back right off, leaving the PowerPoint show freely accessible to her. After Irene has discovered this new source of amusement she can be shown many ways of modifying it which may intrigue her. We will discuss those in detail in coming chapters.

Chapter 3

Telling Your Own Story

Marie

Staff at Marie's care home change regularly and the home often employs 'agency' staff who know little of Marie's past. To help her 'tell her own story' she has been helped by Liz, a support worker at the home, to produce her multimedia 'lifestory' using PowerPoint. PowerPoint is an excellent tool for creating multimedia shows. People tend to remember going to meetings, seminars and conferences and seeing one PowerPoint presentation after another and often think of it as a rather boring programme used with too much text and clipart unrelated to the topic! However, PowerPoint has many features which are not explored to their full potential by most users (Helpsheets A and B). Most people will be familiar with seeing slides in a linear progression – one after another, but will not know that you can add 'buttons' to pages or objects, such as photos, to take the user to a different part of the show (this is explained in more detail below). These features make it an ideal tool to create a multimedia lifestory which can be interactive. The viewer of the lifestory can choose which 'area' of the lifestory they look at and in which order, returning to the beginning whenever they want.

Before Marie was introduced to the computer for the first time, a member of the IT staff was able to set up her Desktop to meet her individual needs. As this was a 'stand alone' computer he didn't encounter the problems which often frustrate people trying to set up accessibility options (Chapter 9) on individual Desktops (when on a network you need 'Administrator' privileges in order to change settings or add programmes). With Marie's failing eyesight Mike from the IT department went through the different colour schemes with Marie to find the one which suited her best. He did this by going to 'Control Panel' from the 'Start' menu, then looking at the options in 'Display'. Marie really liked the option of having the 'Extra Large' font on all the menu boxes. Working with Marie to choose the best set-up for her, Mike realised that Marie found it difficult to find the mouse pointer (cursor) on the screen. This was easily remedied by again going to the 'Control Panel' options and selecting 'Mouse', then changing the mouse pointer to black and enlarging it. Marie was thrilled when Mike added a 'trail' to the mouse pointer as she could now easily follow its movements across the screen. These processes are described fully in Chapter 9 so we won't detract from the story at this point, but it is worth remembering that it is possible to customise a Desktop within the Microsoft operating system.

Marie made full use of all the features of PowerPoint to create her own, very individual lifestory. Before beginning to create the lifestory on her computer Marie was encouraged by Liz to talk about all aspects of her life – the things that happened in the past, her life as it is now and even about her hopes and aspirations for the future. This was done over a period of time, but to help her remember the things they had talked about Liz used graphics and photos to build up a picture of the areas covered. Once they were satisfied that they had a good idea of the areas Marie wanted to include in her lifestory they created a 'storyboard', a graphical image (a bit like a comic strip) of the order and how each area linked with others. Then together Marie and Liz worked on the computer and looked at various colour options for her lifestory. The completed lifestory reveals more about Marie than was first known to Liz and the other staff at the home. Her choice of a very bold colour scheme (blue background and yellow writing) suggest that she isn't as timid as many people think. Her choice of animations and 'voice-overs' reveal more of her character and sense of humour and the way the pages are laid out (with photos in a symmetrical arrangement) show her as a person who likes order and tidiness.

On her front page (similar to a home page on a website) Marie chose to display which 'areas' she wants to access – these include her childhood, her married life, her family, her cat and her hobbies. In order that the user can view the area of choice, rather than having to look at each area sequentially, Marie and Liz added buttons to the front page with the names of the areas. To do this select 'Slideshow' from the menu bar. Then 'Action Buttons' and click on the first option displayed (blank square) (see Appendix 1, hint 1). Now place the cursor on the page where you want the button to appear and drag it out to the desired size. You select the page that you want to appear when the button is pressed in the dropdown menu next to 'Hyperlink to'. The colour of the button is changed by right-clicking on it (i.e. click using the right button on the mouse) and selecting the 'Format Autoshape' option.

Marie owns many photos of her past life and she brought these to the first sessions when deciding how to plan her lifestory. These photos have been scanned in and organised within the different areas (Helpsheet C). Sounds have also been added which will encourage Marie to recall the memories connected to the photos, for example when the page showing her wedding opens the 'wedding march' plays automatically (Helpsheet A). There are many websites which have short audio clips which are invaluable when looking for just the right sound to make a picture more exciting and for creating a truly multimedia lifestory. For example, one photo which Marie is very fond of is of herself surrounded by her family at an outing to the seaside. To bring back the whole atmosphere Liz downloaded the sound of seagulls from a website. She did this by going onto www.findsounds.com and typing 'seagulls' into the 'Search for' option. This produced a choice of 55 different seagull sounds. Liz found Marie's preference and 'saved' it to the computer (a good tip here is to create a folder for all resources used in the lifestory so that you can find them easily (Appendix 1, hint 2)). PowerPoint will prompt the user to decide on the option for playing the sound, i.e. whether it will play automatically when the page is opened (as they chose for the wedding page) or whether the user chooses to play it by clicking on the speaker icon.

When she was asked to record her own voice to describe the photos or memories associated with them, Marie was reticent, so at first the supporter did this for her, though after a while Marie got her courage up and took over. Recording a voice in PowerPoint is a simple procedure on modern computers but it is a feature which is often overlooked even though it is very powerful for people who are unable to read. To do this select 'Insert' from the menu bar, then 'Movies and Sounds' and finally 'Record Sound'. You can then speak into the microphone and your voice (or any sound made) will be recorded. A small speaker icon will appear on the PowerPoint slide and clicking on this will play the recorded message (Helpsheet A).

Marie's family have helped to provide the resources for the lifestory and the grandchildren have recorded their own messages which will play when Marie clicks on their photos. This helps staff to support Marie when she confuses her grandchildren with her own children. Unfortunately, Marie doesn't have a photograph of her cat but she conducted her own 'identity parade' of photos of cats through Google Image Search (Helpsheet D) and she chose one which she thought was her cat. Within her lifestory an animation (downloaded from www.uselessgraphics.com) of a cat and a cat's cry have been added and Marie remembers her own cat with fond memories and can recall his name and some of his antics (prompted as necessary).

Marie is proud of her knitting and is being encouraged to knit dolls' clothes for local bazaars. Whenever she completes a garment a staff member takes a digital photo of it and it is added to a section in her lifestory. She particularly enjoys showing new staff this section and they see that Marie is still able to contribute to the life of the local community. Liz has encouraged staff to take photos of the dolls' clothes on display in the local community shop as Marie loves to see her work on display and being admired by children.

Kumar

Kumar began his lifestory at the special school he attended. This makes introducing himself to new people, including those professionals who are currently
shaping his life, much easier as it includes many of the things he did at school
and brings out his personality in the design. His design is far less 'formal' than
the one chosen by Marie. Kumar likes a mixture of colours with each area having
a different background and text colour combination.

   Because Kumar's lifestory was created in school with minimal input from
his family it is more a record of his 'achievements' and gives no indication of his
dreams and aspirations for the future. He is currently working on this with a
member of staff, Rob, who is working with him on his person-centred plan. He
likes to add animations to brighten his design and chose many of them from
www.clipart.co.uk. Kumar likes horses and although he has never owned or
ridden one he wanted to tell people about his dream of riding in the 'Future'
section of his lifestory. So once he, with Rob's support, had accessed the clipart
website he then chose 'Animated gifs' from the list on the left of the page and
from the long list of subjects he chose 'Horses' and then the animation he
wanted to add to his page. While they were on this site Kumar and Rob explored
many other options for Kumar to include in his lifestory as it evolved. They
followed the advice given to them and saved any animations for future use in the
'Resources' folder which they had created on Kumar's computer (Appendix 1,
hint 2). They didn't want to risk not being able to find the really good
animations they had located.

   Kumar used a computer at his school and has many IT skills which he has
managed to incorporate into his lifestory. Now that Kumar has his own
computer and isn't being told by the school's IT technician that he can't deviate
from the school's standard set up, he has experimented with the background on
his Desktop and has imported a picture he took with his digital camera. It
reminds him of a visit to somewhere special and he enjoys seeing it each time he
switches on his computer. To do this Kumar went to the 'Control Panel' through
the 'Start' menu, just as Mike did for Marie, and he too went to 'Display' and
'Desktop' and discovered the 'Browse' button which enabled him to set any
photo he had on his computer as the background to his Desktop. Kumar wanted
to have a completely different mouse pointer from everyone else and so, while
he had the 'Control Panel' open, he went to 'Mouse' and selected 'Pointers' tab
from 'Mouse Options'. From the dropdown list he chose dinosaur and was
pleased when (after selecting 'Apply') his cursor (mouse pointer) turned into a
pleasant yellow and was even amused when a small yellow dinosaur appeared
on the screen every time the computer was 'busy'.

Now back to Kumar's lifestory. On his front page he wanted the title to be 'Kumar's Lifestory' and he wanted this to be personal to him so he used his knowledge of WordArt to put a photograph as the background to his name. Doing this gives the impression that his name has been cut out of his photo. To do this Kumar firstly clicked on the WordArt button at the bottom of his screen (the one that looks like a capital A tilted to the right). He then selected the style in which he wanted his name to appear by double clicking on it and then in the box which appears he typed in 'Kumar'. Then he selected the name when it appeared on his page and right clicked on it (using the right-hand mouse button). A new menu appeared and he selected 'Format WordArt'. Kumar made sure the 'Colors and Lines' tab was selected by clicking on it. Then he clicked on the down-arrow on the 'Fill Color' selection and selected the 'Fill Effects' option. Next he made sure that the 'Picture' tab was selected and then he selected a photograph of himself from one he had previously stored on the computer (Helpsheet E).

The lifestory is a valuable starting point as it gives the background of and an insight into Kumar's experiences. As Kumar has little experience of using the Internet, together Kumar and Rob are exploring the Internet and learning new skills to research things Kumar might like to do. For example, Kumar is aware of his ethnic background but has little knowledge of the part of Asia his father comes from. He is now researching his family tree which will also be added to his lifestory. This knowledge helps to give Kumar a 'sense of belonging' and he hopes that in future he will be able to share this with his father and maybe his father will help him to add the missing pieces or tell him stories of his own childhood, which Kumar is eager to include in his lifestory.

His sisters are also beginning to see that this is an excellent way to show Kumar as the person he really is and they are scanning in old family photos for him to add to the lifestory. His grandmother has recorded a few sentences in Hindi (her native language) which reminds Kumar of when he was a small child and she used to sing him Hindi songs.

Kumar's lifestory has a very colourful front page. He decided that he wanted the photos he has added to be the buttons to take the user to the different areas of his lifestory. To do this he clicked on the photo to highlight it, then selected 'Slideshow' from the menu bar and then 'Action Settings'. In the text box that appears he chose the 'Mouse click' tab and then selected the 'Hyperlink to' option (by clicking in the circle next to it). Kumar was able to choose which page to link to (that is the page to which the button would take the user) from the dropdown menu. Kumar soon learned that he must include a button on the new pages to take him back to the front page (Appendix 1, hint 3).

Using video clips can help stress a point in a way no amount of talking, description or written words can! Kumar has told his sister, Nita, all about his lifestory and she has discussed with Rob how she can support Kumar with this work. Rob has no experience of using a camcorder and so Nita says she will take on this role and work with Kumar on video which can be used to support his person-centred plan and lifestory. After some experimental work, Kumar himself finds it interesting to replay and examine the video clips showing what he does in his metal work, including his mistakes. He finds he can use the video record as a reflective learning tool to improve what he does and increase his satisfaction. He wants to take control of the camera so that he can get more instructive close-ups; he wants a better camera with better definition! Meanwhile he and Nita sometimes set up a tripod and learn to use the remote control facility on the camera so that Kumar is now filming himself at work, i.e. filming his hands, the solder, the soldering iron and whatever metal assemblage is going on. As we shall see, Kumar goes on to find a lot to do with the video camera.

Kumar and Nita accumulate a fair number of video clips of him at work. They decide to use the simple movie editing programme which came with the camera, i.e. ArcSoft Video Impression (you can purchase other software for editing videos such as Ulead Video Studio or Pinnacle Studio Plus). For the moment we will stay with the free software; using that you can choose what order to put clips into a sequence, but you cannot shorten a clip or embellish it in any way (as you can with the other video editing software previously mentioned). The end result of using ArcSoft is more tightly sequenced and more like a 'real movie' than the result of using PowerPoint as your basic tool for stringing video clips together. ArcSoft – at least in the free versions which come with a variety of makes of digital camera – also has the annoying feature that you have to start again from the beginning if you want to make an insertion or alter the order. Generally it doesn't offer as much flexibility for inserting other material (titles, for example) as PowerPoint. Kumar and Nita, who edit it together, decide to combine short movies (in .avi or .mov format) made with ArcSoft into a PowerPoint show which she will take to the planning meeting, which Kumar firmly refuses to attend, about his life and his hopes of going to college to do A-levels. There has been some opposition to this because of Kumar's tendency to lose his temper when things go wrong and this will not meet the expectations of the tutors.

They string their chosen video clips together to make two short movies. One lasts about seven minutes and shows Kumar successfully and creatively at work, using the soldering iron safely and making a variety of assembled small sculptures. After it they insert a sequence of high quality still pictures of those sculptures, with titles and a spoken description by Kumar of why and how they were made. He makes the voice-overs with a digital recorder (making .wav files) which can then be inserted at will. Nita and Kumar set this show to run automatically. They make a separate (much shorter) movie of Kumar's error making and his mature response to it. That decision is mainly because despite his keen interest in his own mistakes, Kumar is very uncomfortable about other people focusing on those. He would rather this film did not get shown, but he does accept Nita's argument for including it, 'just in case'. So, after a recorded eloquent statement from Kumar about why he should be allowed to pursue his interests at college, he ends with the question, 'Why not?' which comes up on the screen. The next slide will only play if Nita clicks the show onward. Only if someone raises concerns about Kumar's behaviour at this point will she launch the error-making movie they have made.

It turns out to have been a wise decision to include the scenes in which Kumar gets upset but doesn't 'blow it', because the anticipated objections do materialise when the meeting finally happens. Nita initiates the next part of the show in response to those concerns; she and Kumar have set out the argument in their commentaries between 'incident clips'. They include a clip Nita filmed showing Kumar re-playing the video of one of those occasions, focusing in on what has gone wrong, playing it frame by frame, and lucidly explaining to his sister precisely why things happened as they did. The case for Kumar being supported to pursue this interest is conclusively made. Copies of the CD are passed on to all those involved in Kumar's future. Many of the short video clips are incorporated into Kumar's lifestory which is now pretty extensive for someone so young!

Irene

Staff at the day centre decided to use the computer with Irene in an attempt to introduce her person-centred plan. As we have seen with both Marie and Kumar there were certain things which the staff could do to customise the computer equipment for Irene so that when she did eventually take control of the computer herself it would be an easier process. They knew that she would be unable to hold a mouse in her hand because of her tremor, and so they bought her a large trackerball (described in more detail in Chapter 10) and they were able to alter the settings which controlled the movement of the cursor across the screen, so that it was easier for Irene to control. They researched a variety of trackerballs and the one they bought had a button on it which acted as the double-click, which is a really difficult action for most people. The staff felt that this was one action which Irene would not be able to do, even over time, and she would become frustrated by it and not want to persevere with using the computer. They were also able to slow down the speed of the cursor across the screen through the 'Control Panel' in the

'Start' menu and selecting 'Mouse'. They realised that Irene's tremor would also make it difficult for her to use a standard keyboard and they had seen several alternatives in catalogues which have guards to prevent two keys being depressed at the same time. They decided that this was a large investment at this point and decided to delay buying one until they had tried one with Irene. Later they were to discover that their local AbilityNet (www.abilitynet.org.uk) would loan them one so that they could assess whether it was suitable for Irene.

The first attempt at using a computer with Irene was to start a lifestory and the staff hoped that the pictures of things and places with which Irene is familiar would hold her attention. However, Irene would not engage with the computer and held her head down – not even looking at the screen. Then during a music session when the music from Tchaikovsky's *Peter and the Wolf* was being played, Irene smiled as the music obviously awakened memories for her. On further investigation it was discovered that Irene's school had performed *Peter and the Wolf* several decades ago and everyone in the school had had a part in it. *Peter and the Wolf* had always held happy memories for her. One member of staff, Anna, built on this and produced a very simple story of the music using the tunes in PowerPoint. The tale was told in the format of an interactive story. Anna put arrows at the bottom of each page so that by pressing on the forward arrow in the right-hand corner Irene could move to the next page in the story. Likewise she could go back a page by pressing on the backwards arrow in the bottom left-hand corner. Irene could exit at any time by pressing on the 'Exit' button, which Anna included on each page. They were also able to get a touch monitor so that Irene no longer had to interact with the computer through the keyboard (or similar device) but could touch an object on the screen to cause a reaction – in this case play the music or navigate through the pages. To create a button to move to the next page within PowerPoint Anna selected 'Slideshow' from the menu bar and then 'Action Buttons'. This produces a set of button templates and Anna chose the forward arrow one by clicking on it. Then she placed the cursor on the page where she wanted the arrow to be created and dragged it out to the right size. The default 'link' created with this button is to move to the next page so Anna was able to close the menu box without making any further selections. Anna knows that once you have created one button you can copy it in the usual way and paste it to all other pages as appropriate. It will then be added to the page in exactly the same place and look the same. It will also carry with it the same 'actions' – in this case move to the next page (Appendix 1, hint 4).

The *Peter and the Wolf* PowerPoint interactive story was very successful and Irene learned to look at the screen and to touch objects to produce an effect. Anna was then able to extend this to work with Irene to produce her lifestory. She has an area called 'Things I like'. Staff printed photographs from the

Internet and asked Irene which she liked. This activity was repeated in different sessions at the day centre and a picture of Irene's actual likes (not those assumed by staff) was built up. These were imported into Irene's lifestory and when she touches the picture it makes a sound (people cheering, applause or similar).

Irene has no personal photos of the places where she has lived in the past. Therefore, Anna started her lifestory in the present as it was easy to take digital photos of Irene's current home, day-service, doctor's surgery, local shop, etc. This is in contrast to Liz, who began Marie's lifestory from the time of her birth because she had plenty of photos and it is important for Marie to recollect the past and complete the lifestory in a chronological order to give her a greater understanding of the context of events in her life. As Anna builds on Irene's lifestory with her they look on the Internet for photos to fill in the blanks, for example, Irene knows she was born in Canterbury but doesn't possess any personal photos so Anna uses Google Image Search (Helpsheet D) to find photos of Canterbury. This produces 67,000 photos of Canterbury (257,000 if you do not specify 'UK' in your search, showing just how many Canterburys there are outside the UK!) and Irene chose the ones she likes most to put in her lifestory. If Anna comes across more information from friends or family or is lucky enough to be given a photograph, the photos used in the lifestory can be replaced with actual photos.

Irene's lifestory is ongoing – it will take a long time to complete as staff gather more information about her past, but Irene is participating in it at all times and the skills learned are being used to benefit her in other areas. For example, she uses the Internet for researching things other than for her lifestory, recently she looked at holiday destinations and also worked out with staff the best way to travel, using bus and train timetable websites to calculate costs of travel and the most convenient times for journeys.

One of the most important parts of a lifestory, if it is to form part of an individual's person-centred plan is the section for the future which will incorporate hopes, dreams and aspirations. For the staff working with Irene it has always been difficult to understand what Irene might want in her future. This is where the Internet can be used as a 'probe' for getting to know what she finds alluring without anyone having to leave the house. We're not completely ignorant of her likes and dislikes, of course. But both Irene and her carers are confined by their actual rather limited shared experiences. Irene does not usually leave her room to watch anything on the television (perhaps because the staff or other residents dominate channel choice and don't choose what she would choose – we don't know). So television has not been a useful source of clues to what Irene really wants to do. However, as the lifestory developed the relationship between Irene and the staff who work most closely with her changed and she was able to communicate with them more readily. This is often the case when working on lifestories and may be because of the development of a one-to-one relationship over many hours as the lifestory unfolds, and because the focus of attention shifts to the individual who becomes more empowered by the process. In Irene's case it became clear to Anna that what she really wants is to live on her own. This was a real revelation as no-one had ever considered that either Irene wanted this or that it might be a possibility. Working on the lifestory gave Anna the opportunity to explore this more with Irene.

Our 'armchair' preparation means doing some intensive downloading of images and using those to make some more PowerPoint shows. Irene knows by now how these work, she can do things with them. Very easily a set of short shows can be created on various topics, e.g. pop stars, pop songs, films and film stars, waterfalls, local wild life, exotic wildlife, birds, cookery, glasswork, horses, gardens, stately homes, dancing, stained glass windows, church architecture, racing cars. Generally speaking, the less well you know a person the wider your sampling of possible topics of interest should be. People in care often experience poor quality support even when high quality individuals with high aims and principles are at work. Among many possible reasons for that is poor continuity both of staff and of staff access to personal history through the files.

Anna and Irene would spend time looking on the Internet at different types of houses; using Google Image Search (Helpsheet D) Anna was able to show Irene photos of a range of houses, bungalows and flats in an array of situations. They 'discussed' each one until Anna was confident that Irene had a real idea of the type of house she wanted to live in. Determining the location of Irene's ideal home was more difficult. They looked on the Internet for different facilities which Irene might use within the neighbourhood. Through doing this Anna was able to see that Irene did in fact have memories of going to the theatre and cinema, but she did not appear to understand libraries or museums. She liked the idea of small local shops rather than shopping in supermarkets or shopping malls. Irene became excited when they started looking at photos of churches and it soon became obvious that church had played an important part in her childhood and that Irene would like to have a church within walking distance of any potential new home.

Anna was pleased that Irene was able to show her so much about the sort of life she is dreaming of and decided to use the computer to help Irene make more choices. This time they looked at interior decoration. Irene's room is currently painted in the same magnolia colour as everyone else's. This has always been the case in the residential home as it is low maintenance and cost effective to have everywhere painted the same colour. No-one had considered whether the residents would prefer a different décor! Anna used a simple paint and draw package (Paint comes with Microsoft operating systems and can be found in the 'Accessories' folder in 'Programs') and played around with colours with Irene indicating which ones she likes and which she really doesn't like. They talked about the colours Irene likes and which she would like her walls to be and then which colour she would really like for her bedding, curtains, etc. Anna then started taking Irene to visit shops to look at soft furnishings and they had fun saying which they really liked. It was difficult to maintain these outings so Anna went to a computer shop and bought a simple, cheap computer programme (from a choice of several) which allows you to design your home and garden and used this with Irene, changing the colours of walls, carpets, etc. and watching Irene's reactions. The digital camera will now come into its own. It can take video clips of reasonable quality, which can even be played back on a television. It can take high quality still pictures, which can be displayed on computers or televisions as well as being printed out. Anna shows them all to Irene to see if she enjoys looking at them! She chose some pictures in which it is obvious Irene is keenly interested in the topic on-screen. She shares them with Irene's family and copies them to a CD so that they can look at them at home in their own time.

Each time Anna accompanies Irene on the outings to look at interior décor she offers Irene the opportunity to use the camera herself, but she will not do so even after several weeks. Anna films the beginning of the outing each time, with a voice-over saying the date and where they are going that day. A brief shot of Irene using today's mode of transport – walk, bus, or train – will be followed by some longer shots of the place they're going to and of Irene exploring it. Again a voice-over can be a helpful aide memoir later. Finally the return home is recorded and its exact time is stated. All that can be turned into a short movie with 'scene changes' without using anything more specialised than good old PowerPoint once more. You just start a new show. Insert each video clip in the order in which the events recorded happened. Set each clip to play automatically when the slide opens. Insert a title between each clip if wished. This is all done, as much of it as possible with Irene. It is all then saved to Irene's 'Outings' folder with the day's destination as its title. Once Irene has seen how this process works a few times she may be able to carry it out for herself or perhaps only after many more times will she be that confident, or perhaps she never will. *It is important to keep offering her the opportunity, and meaning it. Never stop!* We must not reinforce her long-held, and sadly justified, beliefs about her own lack of efficacy. We have to change those beliefs by introducing her to a reality in which she truly is effective. This simple movie-making is a step in that direction.

After several outings and follow-up sessions, Anna now has a pretty good idea of the sort of home Irene would like and they build this into Irene's lifestory so that she can show this at her next review meeting. They have also included some slides which show the type of home Irene would really like to live in and the things which are really important for her to have within the locality. This is a very powerful way for Irene to get her message across to those professionals who make the decisions about her life.

The method proposed here has potential for giving individual carers a fast-track way to get to know Irene, both during the process of discovery we are describing, and in the long-term record which will automatically result from the process of the lifestory work. Making sure that that record gets accessed must be a priority. The outcome of the process of choice in the shape of a link to the chosen PowerPoint shows should be included in Irene's continuing and developing lifestory. Looking at that should of course be part of the induction process for all staff. However, it is also worth creating a new folder called 'Irene's Favourites' to store her choices, and putting it on the Desktop. Temporary staff, i.e. 'cover' and 'bank' workers who come in when full-time staffing is inadequate for whatever reasons, may benefit from that. Full-time staff have to take a lot on board in their induction, so why not make their life easier too?

Using pictures to make some new shows is really simple, just choose a format and paste in as many good quality pictures as you can find on the topics you guess might possibly be interesting, in this case we are thinking about Irene's choice of house, location, furniture, colour schemes, etc. Give each show a name and then make a sort of 'over-show' with a sample picture from each topic for the first slide. For example, start by making a presentation of a wide range of houses – and another of a wide range of furniture. Then make a show called 'Irene's Choices' in which there is a slide entitled 'Houses' with one or more hyperlinked small images of house types from that show, and there is a slide entitled 'Furniture' with one or more hyperlinked images of all types of furniture, each of which leads to the whole show of that name.

Once that preparatory work has been done, run through all the shows while Irene is around. Demonstrate to her that there is an overview show which she can explore. Show her that all the pictures link to more of the same sort of thing – and encourage her to take control. Although she knows *how to* by now, she may need reminding that she is *allowed to* intervene in these actions about her life. It is important generally to make sure that she knows that she can at any time open and engage with any of her own PowerPoint shows. It is especially important when a planning process is under way, as it is in Irene's case. We are doing person-centred planning with Irene, something no-one has really succeeded in doing before – whether because they couldn't see how or because they didn't see the point.

The next stage in this process is to make a show with the aim of presenting it with Irene in control at her next person-centred planning meeting. The goal will be to make it clear at that meeting that Irene is choosing to go out and about to visit new locations and to look at housing options. It has emerged during her adventures and in her involvement with the video clips that Irene has strong ideas on where she would like to live and wants to live. When Irene presents her lifestory during the meeting, the many assembled professionals who are used to thinking of Irene as a non-participant are deeply impressed. Her own family is amazed. All these people who have a stake in her life are surprised by her calmness, they are surprised that she stays at the meeting, they are surprised that she has been involved in making the multimedia show, they are surprised that she is in control of presenting the show, they are surprised by what they see in the show – and above all they are surprised by this evidence of Irene's intelligence. Irene is treated with new respect. The staff who have been involved in making all this happen are also treated with increased respect. For a while this meeting has the effect of completely flattening out the hierarchy and leaving everyone involved feeling equal to everyone else. Of course that extreme effect doesn't last, but the hierarchy never again seems so steep after that. For Irene and for the staff who've been involved, this PCP meeting is an intensely rewarding event, unlike every other previous meeting of its kind.

Next time the meeting itself will be recorded with a digital camera. Irene has demonstrated that she is happy to be on screen and finds it interesting and rewarding to see herself there. The meeting being recorded is the best possible way of ensuring that Irene and everyone else involved in her life can access and share the person-centred plans about her and about how she chooses to spend her time. A short edited version with the key decision points can be linked to her lifestory, especially the parts about her dreams, hopes and aspirations for her future.

Things to consider when embarking on lifestory work

We have now looked at how our three people have each created their multimedia lifestories. There are some considerations to take into account when working with people to create lifestories. The first and most important one is that it is the lifestory of that individual and belongs to them. They should be involved throughout the whole process. One exception to this may be the technical part, actually putting it all together. Although some people may have the skills or may want to learn the skills, to import lots of photos can be time-consuming and boring and may need to be done by the member of staff.

Not everyone will want their lifestory in a multimedia format, preferring perhaps to have a photo album or scrapbook or even a memory box. However, by scanning in photos or works of art created in a craft session, the originals can remain with the person, but if they get lost or damaged then there is always a permanent backup. Anna is well aware of this danger and so when working on the multimedia lifestory she takes a backup of it and the resources folder and keeps them separate from the computer. She has decided that a good method of backing up work-in-progress is on a memory stick. Once Anna and Irene are happy with what they have achieved, Anna will take a copy on a CD and also give Irene her own copy on CD.

A lifestory is never finished! It is ongoing and should reflect changes in the person's experiences and hopes and dreams. It is time-consuming to start a lifestory of a person who is in his 50s, but then it can be added to regularly to keep it up-to-date. When working with someone on their lifestory be prepared for reminders of bad events to arise as well as all of those good memories and have in place a procedure (both for staff and service users) should anyone need help and support to get through those (sometimes unresolved) issues.

Chapter 4

Asking and Telling

The title of this chapter and a good deal of its content have been influenced by a book authored exclusively by people on the autism spectrum who have themselves learned to speak out. The book is called *Ask and Tell* (Shore 2005) a snappy short title relevant to issues of advocacy, self advocacy and disclosure as well as being a joky reference to the infantilising of people with communication problems, since 'ask and tell' is a popular theme for children's early learning books. Unless and until people can find a way to make an impact on the discourse into which their lives are embedded they will be treated like children and they will be disempowered and de-skilled by being treated thus. That means that we need to ensure people have – and recognise that they have – access to ways of communicating which make the people on whose support they depend sit up and listen.

The analysis of the process of developing self-advocacy skills which is found in *Ask and Tell* applies across the whole field of people receiving institutionalised support. Kassiane Sibley's chapter, 'Help me help myself: teaching and learning self-advocacy' is particularly relevant. In a way this 'Asking and Telling' chapter picks up where *Ask and Tell* leaves off, by adding the potential of information technology to the process. As we have already seen, presenting one's views via a computer is a good way of increasing the chance of being treated with respect.

Kumar is highly aware that in person he is likely to become tongue-tied, especially when asked a question. He knows this inability to communicate under pressure makes him look stupid. Looking stupid and being treated with disrespect make Kumar feel spectacularly upset. When he feels that upset the possibility of effective communication becomes more and more remote. He cannot speak at all at those times. Meetings which are about him, in which he is meant to be the centre of attention, are a nightmare for him: he cannot bear them. They make him feel exposed, helpless, impatient and angry. They are meant to make him feel important, put him at the centre of decisions about his life, and boost his autonomy: they tend to do the opposite.

Kumar's sister Nita, who has done so much to get him to use video constructively, faithfully attends all his meetings. But she doesn't want to be his permanent substitute, and she doesn't want to be thought of as Kumar's spokesperson nor does she want to be relied on by him to be that. She is keen to foster independence in her brother now that he is a young adult. Nita wants to coax him gently towards an eventual goal of self-advocacy. To help clarify what will be involved in this process, she turns to Sibley's chapter in *Ask and Tell*, about teaching and learning self-advocacy.

Nita finds that the very first step proposed is to plan an advocacy action together, which will be carried out by the friend or ally while the individual who is learning how to self-advocate observes. Fully discussing both the content of what is to be said and the best way of saying it is very important. Nita always makes a point of having a good discussion with Kumar about the content of what she should say on his behalf, but she has not thought about helping him understand that how requests are made can make a big difference to how likely it is that they will be satisfactorily answered. Sibley also recommends that how a particular issue has been dealt with should be discussed and analysed afterwards. Nita proposes to Kumar that she should record the next meeting so that he can see how she has dealt with the issues he wants her to raise. They will then be able to replay and reflect at leisure on the way in which Nita has advocated for Kumar and on the apparent effectiveness of her intervention. They rehearse together what Nita will say and how she will say it.

Nita explains to the people attending Kumar's next PCP meeting that he has requested that she make a video record of the meeting. That will be a reliable way of reporting the meeting to its central character. As well as it being a good way for Kumar to get assurance about the issues he has raised, the video record also means that Nita will be able to point out to Kumar that she has remained calm and reasonable throughout the discussion, and that she has listened patiently while other people have spoken.

When Nita brings out her camera at the beginning of the meeting, she is not surprised when one of the professionals present raises an objection on the basis of Kumar's 'confidentiality'. She has already encountered the way in which the concept of individual confidentiality can be invoked to protect staff practices and avoid scrutiny. So Nita has had the good sense to anticipate this objection and has recorded her brother making a short statement about the importance to him of having a record made through which he will be able to understand key decisions about his own life and the reasons for those decisions. Nita replies to the professional's objection by playing everybody Kumar's very clear and definite statement on her laptop. She also offers to give everybody a copy of the resulting film if they wish and/or to play it back to them immediately when the meeting has finished its discussions. The people at the meeting agree to let Nita make an audio-visual record without further demur, only declining to have copies of the film, on the basis of concerns about confidentiality.

Kumar is extremely interested in viewing the meeting about himself now he is safe from the spotlight, and safe from unpredictable alien probes. In the company of his sister he is thoroughly comfortable and able to communicate well, not just because he is more relaxed but because he reckons Nita understands him better than any of the other people who are apparently concerned with his life. Now they can go through the whole thing together, and they can stop and replay any moment which Kumar needs to examine more closely.

The main issue Nita is raising on his behalf at this meeting is that her brother wants to pursue further education – as is his right. He wants to get A-levels – he has GCSEs but soon after he got those his school place stopped fitting him and the bullying overwhelmed him. He will not consider the possibility of lowering his sights and going to a suggested tertiary college which offers courses in daily living skills or weaving to people with learning disabilities. Kumar is extremely resistant at this stage in his life to any suggestion of kinship with those weird folk who can't talk clearly, who dribble, who are 'thick as two short planks' (Kumar collects idioms). Anyway, it's not just his preciousness, he really does want a proper education, he really does want authoritative qualifications.

The trouble is that for Kumar to succeed in a mainstream setting he would need effective one-to-one support throughout his time in college – and that level of support is only funded in his local authority for people who count as having severe learning disabilities. In many areas the 70 IQ, which is referred to in Valuing People (Department of Health 2001), is taken as the deciding line when allocating support and evaluating support needs (despite later government clarification that the figure was not meant to be rigidly applied and should be disregarded in cases of individual need assessment). Although Kumar's local authority is not being rigid and insists it is indeed assessing individuals on the basis of their individual support needs, they still regard him as already very fortunate with his four hours a week outreach support from Rob (intended to keep his finances and personal hygiene on track). Kumar risks falling into the catch-22 trap of being officially too able to need support because he is able enough to do A-levels (if he gets the support). In this respect his unwillingness to attend his PCP meetings acts in his favour.

According to Valuing People, person-centred planning is a process of continual listening and learning focusing on what is important for someone now and for the future: and acting on this in alliance with their family and friends. At this meeting, Nita has stood in for family and friends as well as for

Kumar. Their mother feels her English is not good enough and she is not used to being expected to be assertive so is not willing to go along to these meetings. Their father avoids the meetings because of different embarrassments – acknowledging that he has a son with special needs is almost unbearable for him, even in the privacy of his own home.

As they go through the video of the meeting together, Nita points out who is speaking out in support of Kumar and his educational needs and who is actually undermining his aim while ostensibly supporting it. Kumar finds this very interesting indeed and replays the 'forked tongue' episodes and in particular the introductory disclaimer 'Of course we all recognise Kumar's right to continuing education' until he is 100 per cent certain that Nita's analysis is correct. It is also to be hoped that he has a better idea about how to recognise future examples of bad faith. It is important that he does not take this on as an assumption about everybody in authority. Discriminating between the people who have his best interests at heart and those who do not is a key survival skill. As well as pointing out the couple of apparatchiks whose main job is to reduce expenditure, Nita also points out that both his speech therapist and his outreach worker are clearly 'on his side'. Kumar is pleased and surprised by this, and interested in the concept of having allies in his struggles.

Another point Nita emphasises as they go through the video is that when she is presenting Kumar's point of view she does so steadily and calmly, she does not get agitated when pressed, and she makes sure the argument in favour of Kumar getting sufficient support to further his educational goals is fully and clearly stated. She explains to Kumar that stating the case in this unemotional way means it is more likely to be heard favourably. Nothing has been firmly decided at the meeting except the principle that Kumar does indeed deserve and have the right to study A-levels of his choice. The siblings agree that they will prepare a presentation by Kumar for the next meeting, which is just three months away as Nita has requested. Having had the practice with Rob his outreach worker in using PowerPoint to make his lifestory and represent his interests, Kumar is very happy and confident about this development. Outside the pressure of the actual meeting Kumar will have no problem in stating his case calmly, especially if they rehearse his statement together first.

In the presentation Kumar will state his views to camera and integrate those into a PowerPoint show (Helpsheet A) which will include written statements of the argument. They also plan to include material from a sensory assessment which has been commissioned so appropriate adjustments can be made to the environment to accommodate Kumar's sometimes extreme sensory problems. They think this will strengthen his case for extra support. In the event, the sensory assessment reveals that Kumar has an extremely difficult time coping with the constant flickering of fluorescent lights. They interfere with his ability to concentrate on anything else and therefore to learn in an environment which is lit with them. Nita realises that this may rule out both the local colleges where Kumar might have been enrolled for his A-levels. She checks and discovers that indeed both colleges are lit throughout with fluorescent bulbs. She and Kumar discuss that although accommodations to his needs can be expected, asking a college to completely change the way it provides lighting in every classroom and lecture room he may use could seem a disproportionate response to an individual student's needs. Does this mean that Kumar will never be able to study for A-levels? No! It just means he may not find a college at which to do that; he may need to find a different route towards his goal.

Luckily Kumar is experiencing these challenges in a world much more able to provide alternatives than it was even one decade ago. Kumar can study A-levels through e-learning. This next stage is described by Sibley (in Shore 2005) as 'facilitation and confidence building' and the idea is that the person being advocated for will play a larger role (with support) than at the first, 'planning and modelling', stage. Again, keeping the actual meeting and Kumar separate facilitates his ability to contribute at this stage too. He analyses the key points he wishes to make, discussing each one thoroughly with Nita. There are two central issues they are concerned about now: one, as before, is getting some further education; the other is getting opportunities to meet girls. Using the guidance he has picked up from watching how his sister tackled raising issues at the planning meeting, Kumar writes himself a script and makes a PowerPoint show.

Kumar plans to speak to the camera again, but this time he will directly attempt to create a video which will affect the content of the meeting. He decides to embed the speech into his PowerPoint show after some introductory slides stating the main issues he wishes to bring to the meeting (Appendix 1, hint 7). His sister and he rehearse the speech and practise it until he is not rushing it nor sounding agitated or hectoring while delivering it. Each time they record it and play it back together so that Kumar will fully understand the points Nita makes. He finds this rather irritating but does understand that the reason why Nita is making him work at it this hard is that the way he delivers his speech will make a difference to its impact on the other people at the meeting, in particular Kumar understands that it may affect the likelihood of them hearing what he has to say with a favourable attitude.

The whole process of recording and reviewing and revising and repeating the process again is an eye-opener for him: until now he had neither experienced nor imagined experiencing what it is like to witness (to be 'on the receiving end' of) himself making angry demands. Indeed he had hardly any idea of what sort of impression he generally made because he had hardly any notion of making an impression at all and even less notion of the possibility of taking control over that impression. Even Nita who knows her brother so well is surprised at Kumar's excited self-discovery. One of his discoveries is that he is a good-looking young man, and he inserts a comment to that effect into his speech, saying that he believes if he has the opportunity to meet young women he will probably quite easily find one who likes him since he is unusually handsome. To illustrate the sort of place he thinks he would like to go to meet girls, he includes a clip from the old John Travolta movie *Grease*, with young women and men dancing together with vigorous enthusiasm. (Sadly, in reality this way of getting together with a female turns out to be too noisy for Kumar's sensitive hearing.)

After the section with his speech, Kumar includes some quotations from government documents about disability, inclusion, the right to education, and the right to have rights. Once Nita has tipped him off that such documents exist he discovers all of these on the Internet via Google. He also includes a video clip of a talk he has been to about sensory issues in Asperger syndrome. He makes a title page for it and records his own comments about the impact those issues have on him into the PowerPoint show as a voice-over during the opening frame. After that he talks to camera and sets out the solutions that he and Nita have identified together, presenting these as questions he speaks in a series of clips which are interspersed with written answers. He sets answers to appear with animated emphasis (Appendix 1, hint 8) after each question. Finally, Kumar concludes with a slide into which all the written answers have been pasted. That will stay on screen while the discussion about his proposals takes place when the actual meeting occurs.

Kumar and Nita agree that she should record the whole meeting again, with permission. Until about one hour before the meeting, they are both assuming that Kumar as usual will prefer not to be there. However, as the meeting gets closer he finds he is so excited about it and about how effective his presentation will be that he cannot bear not to be there. This is a surprise to his sister, but to Kumar, once he has had the thought that going to the meeting will be a good thing, it is as though that is what he had always thought. Since he has run through the show many times both for himself and with Nita, he is very confident about it (Appendix 1, hint 9). When Kumar is at his most confident he is at his most able (a general truth!) so they go into this meeting together armed with the certainty that they are very well prepared.

Nita has the camera on as they go in, so it records everyone's surprise and in some cases clear pleasure that Kumar himself is there. As anticipated, everyone is very impressed by his professional-looking show (Appendix 1, hint 7). They also seem to follow clearly the arguments he presents for being allowed to pursue A-levels online, and for seeking some social life outside college in environments in which he might be able to meet young women. Everything goes very smoothly until they reach the discussion stage and people start to ask Kumar questions, because he is badly floored by these. One autistic poem (by Jamie Stuart, unpublished) which begins 'Governing the anxiety of answering questions' might have been written by Kumar. He always feels pinned to the wall and exposed by the expectations which questions thrust upon him. He hates that feeling and its effect on his ability to communicate, which plummets under pressure. This is where Kumar's ability to advocate for himself runs out, he can no longer speak (or write, or think...).

Providently, Nita is able to take over with aplomb from where Kumar left off. They hadn't rehearsed this, they hadn't expected Kumar would be there at all, but his 'neurotypical' sister had no problem in stepping articulately in to save the day. In some ways, since three of the professionals there have barely met Kumar in the past, this mini-crisis is a good thing. Although he feels terrible at the time, this meltdown is a vivid demonstration of his needs. So far, they have been seeing someone who despite his odd intonation and his pedantry is far from conforming to their expectations of a person needing professional, funded, help. Now the professionals concerned with Kumar's 'care package' get to see how disabled he can become when his confidence is punctured and his systems crash.

Thanks to their use of information technology, Kumar and Nita have worked their way through the 'facilitation and confidence-building' stage of self-advocacy, as identified by Sibley (in Shore 2005), to the 'moral-support' stage – and instead of having a 'letter-writing' stage they have created a stage of writing things down in partnership which is computer dependent. Gradually they are moving towards fully fledged self-advocacy for Kumar. When they play through Nita's recording of this meeting Kumar threatens to fixate on the moment when it went wrong. Instead, his sister suggests they analyse it at this calm moment when things are *not* going wrong. Understanding one's emotions after an event like this in which there has been a sudden catastrophic loss of confidence may be hard for anyone. It tends to be particularly challenging for people like Kumar who have Asperger syndrome and may be late starters in the emotion trade.

They re-play, analyse and reflect on the moment at which Kumar's ability to speak out evaporates. Nita thinks that they should be able to get round the problem of Kumar feeling horribly challenged by questions. She suggests rehearsing what it's like to be put on the spot by people's expectations of an answer. However, when she tries out asking Kumar even the most basic of direct questions she realises that she normally takes care to avoid these without being aware that that is what she is doing. His reactions even with his sister are angry and defensive, unless she restricts her questions to ones with Yes/No answers, which he can sometimes cope with; otherwise he clams up every time. In fact he declares that next time he will just stick with the original plan and will not attend the meeting. Nita decides that the best way to help Kumar get past this difficulty is for him to focus on other things for a while.

When Nita raises the topic of how to cope with questions several weeks later, she does so in a roundabout way, suggesting that Kumar should start to use emails in advocating for himself. He is already beginning to use emails for other purposes (see Chapter 5). Nita puts it to him that he could clearly state that spoken questions are an issue for him – he can have the statement on a slide – and request that any question should be given to him in electronic form so that he has time to answer them at leisure when the pressure is off. That is a very important accommodation for Kumar and reignites his willingness to attend the meeting in person. His email address is on the slide too, and just to make sure that nobody goes away from the meeting without it, he designs and prints himself a business card with his contact details on, using the Business Card facility in Microsoft Publisher which is on his computer. He gives one to everybody at the start of the meeting.

With the constructive and enlightened support of his sister, Kumar is well on the way to being his own independent self-advocate. Achieving that sort of enablement is what all caring relationships both personal and professional should have as their fundamental process. People naturally do it for each other all the time without even noticing, but it may take a lot more conscious work when one of the parties is on the autism spectrum. We've been seeing how helpful the use of the multimedia potential of information technology can be in this process for an articulate and obviously able young man like Kumar. But Irene may be more of a challenge – people certainly expect her to be challenging!

As we know, Irene does not speak, and over the years she has generally not given the impression that she is paying attention to the speech going on around her. But various support workers over the years have wondered how much she really understood, suspecting it might be a good deal more than Irene usually let on. Since computers and videos have been introduced into her life she is much more readily recognised as an intelligent being and a real person. Everyone who works with her in her house and at the day centre knows that her lifestory is on the computer, and everyone at home knows that these days Irene spends regular time each day happily exploring her calendar (Chapter 9). Using the mouse, she knows how to find her way back and forth between the calendar and her lifestory or her current goals, all of which are hyperlinked to each other.

Irene and Anna, her key worker, have a fun time together assembling favourite clips from places Irene loves into a PowerPoint show which Irene insists must be added to her lifestory presentation (Chapter 3). Irene likes running through her lifestory and has become happy to share it with her care workers, especially whenever a new or temporary support worker comes in. Then it is their obligation to get to know her by looking at her lifestory and they are also trained to write a daily log with Irene into her calendar (Chapter 9). This is another shared experience which she has begun to actively enjoy. Staff who previously have had a lot of difficulty initiating a relationship with Irene now find it a whole lot easier, partly because she has become more obviously willing to engage with them and partly because they have become more obviously willing to engage with her. The computer environment suits both parties and creates a mutual accommodation to each other's needs.

At the meeting in which Irene presents her lifestory for the first time, with her latest aspirations, namely wanting to live on her own, which includes video clips as part of it, the outside professionals are especially impressed and surprised. Those who have been at earlier meetings and witnessed Irene's apparent disregard for the whole procedure are particularly amazed. She is calm, involved, and in control. What is more, when they are scheduling the next meeting, Irene opens her calendar to the right date, though does not herself enter in the information. The speech and language therapist at the meeting is particularly impressed and suggests that PowerPoint could be used to develop writing for Irene as well as picture use (Chapter 5). So far, although Irene will use the mouse to move the slides on, she has herself used the keyboard only once – to remove the 'drama therapy' class from her schedule – and remains dependent on full support to make changes in her schedule.

The fact that Irene does not use the keyboard becomes a topic of discussion, during which Irene neither seeks to participate nor becomes restless. Although she doesn't give any clear sign that she is listening, the fact that she sits still and remains quiet during the discussion strongly suggests that she is listening throughout. Her key worker, Anna, proposes that everyone can see how empowering the computer has been for Irene, and suggests that if Irene could be encouraged to use the keyboard there would be a lot more she could do to express herself and her hopes and needs. A keyboard which could be carried easily and accessed outside for communication purposes is also mentioned. It is decided that encouraging Irene to take control of the keyboard and not just the mouse should be a goal for her 'personal plan' with a timescale of 'as soon as possible'.

Anna also raises the issue that Irene is meant to be the centre of a PCP process in which family and friends as well as professionals are involved. At the moment, Irene has no family, and no friends without a professional connection. In spite of all Anna and Irene's useful work together, in the long run Irene needs other friends than her key worker, who will inevitably move on (or be changed by management decree). Irene is not so content to listen to this discussion, and she leaves the meeting at this point. The meeting decides that if Anna can find a suitable supportive friend/ally/advocate for Irene on a voluntary basis, that will be a good thing, especially someone who is willing to make a long-term commitment.

After the meeting, Anna sums up the decisions which have been made at it and puts them into Irene's lifestory with symbols as well as words, using colour Widgit Rebus symbols (from Widgit Software Ltd) as these are the symbols used at the day centre Irene attends. She goes through it with Irene, makes a point of emphasising the written word when she goes through the decisions with Irene, and says the text out loud while pointing at the letter sequence. Anna thinks Irene may be more drawn to the writing than the pictures, in spite of what she has heard about autistic people liking pictures. She has observed that Irene appears to recognise the names of days of the week on her calendar. Unfortunately, Anna does not find it easy to find the time to explore these possibilities. She decides to prioritise tracking down a suitable friend for Irene who will have confidence at the computer and be willing to encourage Irene to develop her own keyboard skills.

Meanwhile, Kumar's explorations of the Internet (Chapter 5) have led him to some new discoveries. He has discovered other people with Asperger syndrome, and made some email pals. He and the other 'Aspies' have been conversing about how hard it is to get a job, and about how useful it can be to have voluntary work on your CV. Anna identifies this email group as a potential source of the e-learning mentor-cum-ally she is seeking for Irene. When she posts a message wondering if someone in their area might be interested in playing that role, it is Kumar who emails her back.

When he first started using the Internet Kumar was given some very clear rules about using it, based partly on common sense, partly on the straightforward advice on the website www.spired.com. Rob and Nita both advise Kumar against using chat rooms at all, they advise him against registering for Adult Only websites, and they advise him against downloading photos of people of any age who are not fully clothed. All this advice is for his own protection – Rob knows of a case of a young man with Asperger syndrome winding up in jail because he downloaded pictures of young children that were deemed pornographic. The young man was not aware that that was what he was doing, he had problems distinguishing these images from the half naked young bodies which we see everywhere. It is also agreed with Kumar that Rob and/or Nita can check his Internet history from time to time. They could treat Kumar as a child and download protective software, e.g. from www.download.com, but they appreciate that he is not a child and decide not to take that option.

The Spired website makes it clear that there is

> [o]ne important rule to remember when you're on the Internet. Don't give your personal details to anyone unless you're sure you can trust them.... If you do decide to meet an online friend in real life, it is ABSOLUTELY VITAL that you go to the meeting with a friendly, responsible adult. If they really want to be your friend, they won't mind meeting you when other people are around. In fact, it should make them more comfortable; after all, all they know about you is what you've told them. (spired.com 2005)

So before Kumar replies to Anna's request, he talks it through with Nita and Rob. They praise him for checking in with them, and have a discussion with Kumar about how to proceed which concludes that it would be a good start to tell Anna he is interested in principle, and go on from there.

Anna herself is of course very aware of how vulnerable Irene is and how potentially dangerous Internet connections can be when they are acted on in the real world. They have agreed that whoever takes on the advocacy role with Irene will have to have a Criminal Records Bureau (CRB) check, and she explains to Kumar that she will need to start the process off. If you are an individual volunteer, you cannot apply for your own check directly. The organisation the volunteering is for needs to be registered and will make the application for you. Goodfolk, Anna's employers and Irene's service providers, are registered with the Criminal Records Bureau, so Kumar agrees to send Anna his details which she forwards to head office to get the process going. Meanwhile, she goes round to his home to meet Kumar in person, timing the visit to coincide with one of Rob's two-hour sessions. The address Kumar lives at sounded vaguely familiar to Anna, and when she sees Rob she realises why. She has worked with Rob in the past and it turns out that Kumar is in one of the outreach projects supported by Goodfolk, the very organisation for which she works herself! She and Kumar and Rob have a good talk and Anna leaves feeling immensely reassured that Irene will be in good hands and that connecting her with Kumar is not a high-risk venture. Rob speaks very highly of Kumar's character and resolve.

Irene lives just a bus ride away from Kumar, and Kumar loves bus rides. Now it is his turn to use Sibley's 'Help me help myself: teaching and learning self-advocacy' (Shore 2005) for guidance in developing the relationship. But the idea is to go slow anyway, and to keep getting to know each other a bit more by exchanging emails before meeting in person. Anna involves Irene in this discussion from the start; she gets Kumar to email a photo and he finds he is interested in knowing what Irene looks like too, so asks for a photo of her.

Before Kumar can become a useful advocate for Irene in the sense discussed above in which a goal of *self*-advocacy is always clear, he needs to make a personal connection with her and build up a relationship of trust. Their exchange of pictures extends to pictures of where they live – initiated by Anna – which of course suits Kumar very much since he has taken digital photos of every room in his house and of the house from the outside. They go on to exchange maps of where they live from www.multimap.com – initiated by Kumar. Anna informs Kumar that Irene uses PowerPoint, so he pastes into a slide a pair of close-up maps, captured via 'screen grabs' (Appendix 1, hint 10) – one of his immediate neighbourhood, one of Irene's, each found via its postcode. Then in the next slide he uses the screen grab for two more maps when he has zoomed out enough that his local map and Irene's local map can be seen to have overlapping zones. Then in the third slide he zooms out so far that both of their homes can be seen on the same map. He decides it will be better if both homes are marked with coloured circles on that final map, and works out how to do that by inserting an object of the right sort from the 'Drawing' toolbar (Appendix 1, hint 11). Irene appears to really appreciate this sequence of maps and clicks her way through it several times looking keen and happy.

Anna asks Irene if it would be OK to make a short clip of her looking at the successive maps, and she agrees. They send it to Kumar – Irene observing the whole process with keen interest, as she has been throughout the email exchange. Anna repeatedly suggests to Irene that she could take control of this process. She thinks it should be possible for Irene to generalise from her use of the mouse for running through and exploring PowerPoint shows to being able to click on the attach button or the send button. However, Anna is only there part of the time and even when she is there rarely has very much time to spend on this. So, although Irene is around and paying some attention when Anna is exchanging emails with Kumar, she doesn't get enough encouragement at this stage to move on to using the mouse in the new context to do a different job. Irene needs someone who will be willing to spend the time; she needs Kumar, if he has the patience.

So, Irene and Kumar have some connection with each other before they actually meet. And during the connecting they develop a mutual interest in meeting in person. Since St John's, one of the churches which Irene most likes to visit is about half way between them (clearly visible near the edge of both their maps) Anna asks Irene if she'd like to meet Kumar there and Irene agrees. That is not so easy for Kumar since he has never been into a church before. To Anna's excitement, when Irene hears that this is an issue for Kumar, she immediately accesses the pictures of St John's which are linked to her calendar. Anna tells Irene that she has had a very good idea, and Irene watches with satisfaction while the pictures are emailed to Kumar.

In the event, they arrange to meet in a café near the church. Kumar brings with him a folder full of coloured print-outs of the various pictures of the church, and of one of the maps. He doesn't have a picture of Irene with him though he can recall the photo Irene emailed him at the beginning of their email exchanges, but they are both punctual and arrive at the café almost at the same moment. Irene is very pleased to see the pictures. After they have had a cup of tea together – during which Anna has done almost all the talking – the three of them go together into St John's, with Anna pointing her camera and Kumar pointing his!

That meeting is another step in a relationship which progresses unexpect-edly well. Kumar had always been anxious to dissociate himself and his diagnosis of Asperger syndrome from the weird people with 'real learning dis-abilities' who he has always thought of as grunting and dribbling. Like his parents and grandparents, he associates disablement with 'just deserts' for bad karma built up in previous lives. In this cultural background widespread prejudices found across most cultures are given formal support. However, Kumar is also a creature of the twenty-first century, and just like the rest of the world, he is favourably impressed by Irene's happy use of PowerPoint. As a result he finds it easier to relate to her as a real person on an equal footing with himself, rather than as a potential source of pollution which does not belong in the same space as him.

Kumar's getting to know Irene coincides with his increasing involvement in Internet autistic politics. He moves a long way from his original position of assumed superiority, thanks to this dual exposure. Kumar is reading the statements at www.autistics.org and those are having a powerful mind-opening effect, for example teaching him not to equate continence with intellectual ability. At the same time Kumar is finding his respect for Irene's intelligence and understanding is naturally increasing with further acquaintance. His commit-ment and willingness to spend time with her also increase.

Kumar is determined to take Irene as far as possible along the path towards self-advocacy he has followed himself. The next step along this path is getting Irene to use the keyboard – the main reason why Anna looked for a friend for Irene in the first place. So far she has still not even used the mouse for anything but clicking around her calendar or showing her lifestory. Having acquired a laptop, Kumar brings it round to Irene's house and is able to set it up for Internet connection; there is a broadband connection available as this has already been installed for the admin computer in the home. He sits down beside Irene and shows her on his laptop the pictures of the church she sent him prior to their first outing. They both enjoy running through the pictures on their twin screens, timing their progress to keep almost perfectly synchronised. Then Kumar shows Irene a website (www.symbolworld.org) which has been especially developed for adults who are symbols readers and has an online magazine called eLive, full of interesting and topical issues. Irene is very familiar with these symbols as they are in regular use at her day centre.

Kumar makes a short PowerPoint show with a symbol on each page, so that when you run through it, it says 'Shall We Have a Cup-of-Tea? Or something else?' It culminates in a slide with a choice between tea, coffee, milk and water symbols which Kumar has made into hyperlinks (Helpsheet A and B). Each symbol has the word it represents typed in beneath it, and both symbol and word hyperlink to a photograph of the object they symbolise, e.g. to a picture of a cup of tea. Irene sees him making the show but does not respond as though it is addressed to her. Kumar sends it to her as an email attachment and within minutes it has arrived on her computer, which is set to do regular email pick-ups (although this is not strictly necessary when using broadband). Kumar and Irene both notice it arrive as the computer gives out a sound, and Kumar asks Irene to open it, but she looks away and does not make a move towards her mouse. So then he asks her if it's OK for him to go to her emails and open it. Irene's response to that is to alter her body posture in a way which suggests she might be making room for Kumar do that. He tentatively reaches across to her computer and uses the mouse himself to reveal that he has successfully sent her the PowerPoint show. He then has the grace to back off and see if Irene takes back the control and open the newly arrived show – which she does.

Kumar is excited to see Irene clicking her way through his little attempt at communication, and waits with bated breath to see if she will choose one of the options he has put on the last slide. At first she just circles through all the choices. Kumar becomes a bit frustrated during this and he urges her to choose one of the options. Irene continues for some time to keep opening the different choices, apparently ignoring Kumar's encouragement to settle on one. Then, leaving a picture of a cup of tea on the screen, Irene turns round and heads off towards the kitchen. Kumar reckons his experiment has been a partial success and goes to join her for tea in the kitchen.

Irene of course knows that getting her to use the keyboard has been inserted into her personal plan 'for Irene's own good' or 'in Irene's best interests'. She has heard these phrases before and they do not bring out the best in her. She appears to associate them with people trying to make her do things she doesn't want to do. Kumar, or someone, is going to have to be resourceful if Irene is to be enticed into typing. For several weeks Kumar gives up trying to do that, but he keeps sending her emails – and receiving emails back (thanks to Anna) – and he keeps taking along his laptop when he visits, with stuff on it he thinks will appeal to Irene. By a stroke of good luck during this time he discovers some useful items from one of his chat groups with some follow-up links (Chapter 5).

One thing that Kumar discovers is that someone with whom he has been corresponding on the Internet does not speak, even though she writes long, clear, grammatical sentences and deploys a wide vocabulary. She urges him to go and look at www.gettingthetruthout.org – a link from autistics.org which he had not yet followed up. There, he is shown pictures of that site's autistic and immensely articulate author – who looks to him unnervingly like Irene. It makes him question his own assumptions – he had thought he was now immune from prejudice having overcome his initial distaste towards relating to someone who does not speak. It also makes him realise how much more Irene could communicate (a) if she had a communication board which she could always have with her and (b) if she was using a keyboard to type words. The net effect is that Kumar is keener than ever to entice Irene into using a keyboard, and he reckons that he has a good starting point in the possible communication board, which would have no mouse, and only keys. Later on Kumar goes through the whole of *Getting the Truth Out* with Irene, reading out each slide and making comparisons with her own life.

At Irene's next PCP meeting, Kumar attends as her friend and ally. He is far less intimidated by doubts when it comes to defending someone else's interests than when needing to defend his own. They have gone and looked at communication boards together, with Anna, and pictures of the available options have been put into a special 'communication devices' show – which includes pictures of Irene at the computer and Irene showing an interest in the various boards. When asked to describe the pros and cons of the three boards Kumar is proud of his forethought in anticipating this question, and moves on to an analysis of the virtues of the two cheapest ones, which he has prepared as a series of slides in advance, after discussion with Anna. They both go to the meeting wearing T-shirts with the big slogan: 'Not being able to talk is not the same as not having anything to say' (see Chapter 6). Wearing your views so that everyone can see them is one of Kassiane Sibley's ideas (in Shore 2005) that particularly appeals to Kumar, and Irene seems enthusiastic too.

At every opportunity, Kumar emphasises to Irene that words are better than symbols (for most people! – because they are common currency, unlike the specialised symbol systems). He also notes that she sometimes reacts to written words as though she understands them. Reading around on the Internet he discovers that the autistic cognitive style – which to some extent he shares – is typically monotropic or attention-tunnelled (www.autismandcomputing.org.uk). That means that when Irene notes and processes what is going on, she is likely to process each experience she has as a whole or a chunk, not as part of a larger whole nor as being itself made up of parts which could make up different wholes. Learning to understand those possibilities of connection and meaningful relationship is likely to take longer in someone who is extremely attention-tunnelled, as most autistic people are. But it can be done!

The other neat idea Kumar encounters is that of using PowerPoint to encourage people to read. The study he has found (Coleman-Martin *et al.* 2005) uses a specialist programme for this purpose, but Kumar realises he can easily create a PowerPoint show with the key features built in, i.e. simple words with sounds which match their letters closely (even in English with its crazy spellings); breaking the words down into their letters; and making the sound come on when the letter is clicked. For example you could have the letters written and spoken one at a time: c...a...t. Then the letters all appear together on one slide and you click the word and hear 'cat' being said, followed by a short, pleasing, video clip of a cat washing itself. To find out if this project inspires Irene to become interested in writing and thus acquire the potential to speak out in a way anyone can understand, see the next chapter.

You may be wondering what's happening to Marie? Doesn't she also need encouraging towards self-advocacy? Well, in Marie's house they have weekly meetings, as they do in Irene's. But unlike Irene, Marie needs no encouragement whatever to speak out, and often has a list of points she wants to make (and ticks off as she does so to keep herself on track). Marie has always been a forthright person. To find out how she is further empowered by the Internet, read on.

Chapter 5

Connecting and Exploring

Email is Marie's first contact with the wonders of the Internet. Her daughter Rose who moved to Australia has been urging her for some time to start using email as soon as possible. Rose is not too good at keeping in touch with letters and is not chatty on the phone (anyway phones and even stamps are expensive) but she uses emails a lot – and she uses a digital camera which means that with email she could easily send her mum photos of the grandchildren, pets and so on almost every day (at no extra cost whatever). Marie has had Rose's email address neatly but pointlessly entered into her leatherbound address book for some time. Now she acquires an email address of her own and Rose's address gets put where it can be used at last.

Making her lifestory (Chapter 3) had a big effect on Marie's willingness to use her computer – that process got her over the hurdle of being afraid to use a computer at all. Now Marie learns fairly quickly that clicking on the icon of an envelope on her Desktop will open her email. And she learns to look along the top bar to see her options, e.g. 'Create New', 'Send and Receive' and 'Attach' or 'Insert' – all self-evident in their meanings. Once she has sent and received emails with some support a few times she can follow the process without help. Soon she is in touch with her other children by email – even Joanna, who lives just a few miles away – and she is directly exchanging emails with one of her grandchildren.

Marie has albums of family pictures going way back. Her eyesight means that she can hardly see these any more and Joanna has the bright idea of getting her mother a scanner. Together they start scanning them in, labelling each with a date and creating a new folder for each album: 'Family pictures 1937–1950' is the first one. Scanning them into her computer means Marie can send as many copies of photos as she wants, at no cost. An important added bonus from Marie's point of view is that each picture is now displayed in a large format, and is bright and highly visible. She sends all her favourites to everyone in her address book (at this point that is only family). So that Marie can carry on scanning in pictures independently, to make sure that she doesn't lose the thread of the necessary sequence Joanna writes down the steps on a card. At this point in her life, no matter how often Marie successfully negotiates those steps (Helpsheet G) she likes to have an external guide because she so easily becomes unsure of what's meant to happen next. A member of staff laminates the card, punches a hole in its side and attaches it to the scanner. Because her memory for long ago is so strong, many of the photos trigger a stream of recollection – which Joanna urges Marie to write down. Almost every picture she sends is accompanied with an anecdote about the people and places it shows. The stream of emails turns into a historical as well as personal record.

Marie's passion for knitting is what gets her involved in using the Internet beyond email. During all the time that she's been knitting, Marie has spread out whatever she's knitted to display the garment for a photograph before passing it on to the person for whom she's made it. Each photo was put into a special album and labelled. Although she's an amateur, Marie knits to a very high standard and has made a wide variety of challenging and colourful pieces. She is proud of all this work, and the appreciation it receives. Instead of leaving the album unlooked-at on her shelf she has decided to put it into a presentation. Marie painstakingly scans in every one of the photos from her album of knitting.

As she scans the pictures of her knitting onto her computer Marie makes a folder to put them in and calls it 'Knitting Display'. She names each one by its date and whom it was for – again reproducing the information carefully recorded in the album – and saves it into the Knitting Display folder. Now she would like a bit of help to create her own PowerPoint show. Marie has been shown how to do this a couple of times. As with the scanner, her problems with registering new information mean that she needs a few prompts each time. But, unlike using the scanner, using PowerPoint (Helpsheets A and B) means that you are given prompts whenever you need them without having to rely on outside help either in the shape of an external prompt list or of another supportive person.

If Marie looks at her Desktop, among the few icons on display is the one which will open PowerPoint when you click it. Once PowerPoint is open, the option to create a new show pops up on the screen – again just requiring to be clicked. Marie is reminded that it is a good idea to give the new file created a name and save it to a folder and she saves it to her Knitting Display folder, under the title 'Marie's Knitting Show'.

Choosing the right slide format will make Marie's life easier (Helpsheets A and B) – she prefers the title with picture combination from the slide layouts offered but is annoyed by how big the script gets in the title box in that format. She can't work out how to fix that without help – but once she has been shown how, she learns to look for the word 'format' and use that as her start-off point. That either gets her into the 'Format' menu or into the 'Formatting' palette in

Apple Mac. Either of those routes will work even though she only applies them ad hoc, i.e. one slide at a time (Appendix 1, hint 12). In the end she changes her mind and turns each title into a hyperlink to the picture it describes (Helpsheets A and B, also below, this chapter). This is a process she went through while making her lifestory. Marie needs prompting to remember the right word – 'hyperlink' – for this process, but once she has remembered that she can follow the instructions easily. She programmes the picture to 'fade in' each time (Appendix 1, hint 7). To help her through these processes Marie uses a worksheet like those (Helpsheets A and B) in the appendix, laminated for longer usefulness.

The end result is a very professional-looking show, and a really impressive catalogue of decades of work, displayed to its best advantage. Marie wants to let everyone in her family have copies. It makes a very large file to upload so it is explained to Marie that the best way to save it will be to put it on CDs, then these can be sent all over the world and played on computers of every sort. With a bit of help Marie learns the procedure for making a CD (Helpsheet F).

One of the support workers, John, who takes photos, likes to upload them to a website called Flickr (www.flickr.com). At no cost and with no obligation you can sign up and display several of your favourite pictures there (you don't get pestered with messages from them either). You can also have your photos available within several categories, e.g. fungi, bad signs, knitting, while they remain as part of what can be seen at your own Flickr page. That means that as well as your own family and friends seeing your pictures other people who share your special interests also do so. You also have the opportunity to leave messages about pictures and thus connect directly with the people who've taken them. John realises that this would be great for Marie and her knitting pictures and introduces Marie to the site.

There are some other online services offering free picture display, such as Yahoo (which now owns Flickr!) and shutterfly.com but they tend not to have the extremely undemanding and user-friendly qualities which distinguish flickr.com. John shows Marie the site and helps her join up and create a little icon for herself. She uploads several of her favourite knitting pictures (and a couple of family pictures too) up to her (quite generous) permitted monthly total. When looking at her pictures she is given the opportunity to place them in a group. John shows Marie how to find the knitting group and join it. She is delighted to discover so many other photos, in some cases photos of patterns she has knitted herself. In her next upload she looks through her album to find coincidental matches with what's already on flickr.com's knitting display and realises that just two people are responsible for all the overlap with hers; they get in touch. For all the pictures she posts to the knitting group she makes notes about the patterns from which she was knitting and the year. In the many cases when she can remember where she found the pattern, Marie also notes that. As with the family pictures, what Marie is doing is creating a bit of history – this time it is history in a rather specialised but actually public realm.

All these explorations of the past are a special pleasure for Marie because she knows her brain is working not just well but exceptionally well when she recollects distant events. Trying to remember the names of the various support workers who visit her house is a far greater challenge – she is aware of that and frequently feels annoyed with herself because of it. An unexpected bonus of the knitting history at flickr.com is that she makes a couple of new friends, starting off by exchanging comments then exchanging email addresses. They turn out to have more in common than knitting. An unexpected bonus of the personal history arises because one of Joanna's children has a school history project. He uses his grandmother's information to compile an illustrated history of his family in that neighbourhood over three generations. His teacher is extremely pleased with the work, and realises the boy has an interesting grandmother with real depth of local knowledge. The teacher is a member of a local history society and he gets in touch via Joanna, inviting Marie to give a presentation to the society. Now Marie's knowledge of PowerPoint will be used for the purpose for which the programme was originally designed, giving a public show. As we've said, she is not shy in a group, and she takes on this project with relish.

Far from being isolated in her new situation, Marie has found new ways of connecting and new people to connect with since learning how to use the computer. She is communicating much more often with her family and is a bit of a star at the local history society. These threads come together when Marie learns there about Genes Reunited (www.genesreunited.com). She carefully writes its name down in the notebook she always carries as her aide memoire. Marie decides to follow up her own family tree and see if she has any living relatives she doesn't know about. She knows the routine now of entering a URL into Internet Explorer, pressing 'Enter', and getting an almost instant result (though like most people she will probably never understand how). Marie is also delighted also to discover Friends Reunited (www.friendsreunited.com) because she has been remembering so vividly her days at school, and recalls several names of people with whom she lost touch decades ago. Kumar, who learned about the Genes Reunited website while he was creating his lifestory, begins to explores it on Irene's behalf. He has learned that Irene was one of a large family with whom she has completely lost touch.

Like Marie, Kumar's first experiences of the Internet were with email, but he moved on rapidly and by now has become something of an expert on its possibilities where they suit him. He is a frequent visitor to two or three discussion groups and well known for his contributions to those. There he is treated with a respect he tends not to get in the offline world. His poor social timing, his shy hesitancy alternating with torrents of words, is not a handicap online. There, nobody can hear his flat uninflected voice or observe his avoidance of eye contact. There, his fundamental competence is not in doubt.

Kumar has registered to do two A-levels online, maths and computing. They are both subjects he is good at and feels confident in, but he finds keeping to the deadlines extraordinarily hard. He decides he needs to find a way to remind himself in good time of all his deadlines so he spends some time seeking for 'program reminders – free download', on Google. Of course, Kumar could have chosen to set reminders in Microsoft Outlook but he thought this was a very boring way of getting his reminders. He would really like to get a personal digital assistant (PDA), an electronic hand-held information device, and then he would put all of his appointments as well as the due dates for his assignments into this. He could then synchronise the PDA with the computer and automatically have pop-up reminders.

Meanwhile, his Google search finds him some promising links including one to www.freedownloadscenter.com where he has already spent a lot of time exploring. He 'bookmarks' it, that is he clicks on the 'Favorites' button in his web browser and then clicks 'Add to Favorites' (Appendix 1, hint 19). After that, whenever Kumar is looking for a useful piece of free software, that is where he goes first; someone also recommends www.tucows.com – another freeware and shareware site – and he marks that as a favourite too. The fact that it's possible to find so much that's completely free entrances Kumar – he is not rich and has been having his awareness raised about counting his pennies. However, he is missing his A-level coursework deadlines while he makes these delightful discoveries, and he needs to focus his mind on dealing with that issue.

The software with programmable reminders which Kumar has downloaded turns out to be too fiddly and not effective at persuading him to pay attention to the deadlines which they are supposed to flag up. He decides he needs to find a way of sending himself email messages about this – since he knows he pays attention to his emails. He enters (in quotes so it will search for the whole phrase) 'send email messages to myself' into Google, hoping to come up with something. But all he gets is a few mentions of people checking their system is in working order. This quest obsesses him rather. As it happens, Kumar's birthday is around now, and his sister Babli, who has now married and moved away from home, sends him a very charming ecard – that is, an electronic greetings card. Unlike the paper sort these are often animated, usually cost nothing, and can be sent to as many people as you wish at no extra cost.

The card from Babli is Kumar's first ecard, he didn't know they existed till now. It gives him the idea that he could send himself ecards on pre-programmed dates to remind himself about his deadlines. So Kumar sets out to investigate what's available. His Google search finds a great many offers of free ecards and he visits several of the sites and browses their collections. Some sites, such as www.123greetings.com allow you to 'personalise' the cards you send very fully. You can choose not only a card design and inserted message but the card's background colour, and its font colour, size and type. Although Kumar is impressed by these possibilities he finds most of the cards crude and unappealing, and feels overwhelmed by the choice. Also, he finds it hard to take the sprinkling of incessantly animated images on most of these sites – his sensory issues mean that these are excessively distracting. What is more, on many sites he finds the advertising irritating and intrusive.

In spite of those drawbacks Kumar reckons that getting himself sent timely ecards is the right method for keeping himself on track with his A-levels. So he decides to go ahead and choose a bearable card to send himself, and starts the process of making it happen. To his great annoyance at the first site he tries to actually send himself a card it won't even let him programme more than one date for a card to be sent. At another he finds he can only programme cards to be sent up to two months ahead and he wants to be able to do it over a much longer time period than that. Having spent a lot of time by now in pursuit of this aim, Kumar feels extremely frustrated by these experiences. However, it leads to an interesting discussion with his sister about the meaning of the expression 'there's no such thing as a free lunch'.

As a fairly typical person with Asperger syndrome, when Kumar has heard this expression about free lunches before, he has taken it at face value. Kumar thinks it is simply untrue: he knows he has had many a 'free lunch'. When he complains to Nita that he is getting really annoyed with all these sites offering free ecards, she says 'There's no such thing as a free lunch', and suggests Kumar should go to the site Babli sent her card from, and pay. Kumar has been resolutely pursuing all the irritating free offers but ignoring the possibility of paying. As we've said, he has been firmly told that he needs to be careful with his spending: Kumar takes this very seriously indeed and worries about every bit of spending he does. He is afraid in case he runs out of money. He declares to Nita that there is indeed such a thing as a free lunch – and he has no intention of paying for a service he can have for nothing.

Nita tells Kumar that everything which takes work has somehow to be paid for, *directly* or *indirectly*. She suggests they sit down together and take a look at one of these 'free' sites together and try to work out what actually pays for them. The clue is the advertisements which of course are their essential source of revenue, and advertisers are actively solicited on these free sites. If you look at the 'small print' on most of these sites you will find a place where you can click to find out how to advertise and what the advantages to you will be if you do so. On one ecard site Kumar and Nita find advertisers being offered space in newsletters and email messages, and/or in banners, tags and links all over the site. On 123greetings.com – one of the oldest and best respected sites – they find this statement of the key selling points of advertising space in this location:

> advertisers on 123greetings.com get a unique platform to reach out to a focused audience that is loyal, receptive, and e-commerce-friendly.

> **High Volume and Reach**
> With over 240 million impressions a month and an ever growing list of users, 123greetings.com is one of the premier sites on the Net to reach your customers.

> **Active Audience**
> While TV ads address a captive audience, online ads target an active audience. 123greetings.com scores over most other sites in this respect as visitors to the site are actively engaged in viewing, selecting and sending ecards and our interactive content makes them more receptive to advertising messages. Our sponsors can forge an emotive link with our users by establishing an association with the positive feelings generated by popular festivals/events. (123greetings.com 2005)

This is all a revelation to Kumar. But the bit that really gets to him is the concept of an 'emotive link' (a new idea to him) and worse still the possibility that such a link could be forged in order to make someone more likely to buy something. He finds this shocking and rather disgusting along with the implication that people's 'loyalty' may be exploited for profitable purposes. Kumar is becoming less naive; this is very distressing for him though a normal part of growing up. The end result of this discussion and exploration is that – at least in this context – Kumar has a good idea of what is meant by 'there's no such thing as a free lunch'. That means he is more willing to stump up some money for a service that does not have any of the many features that disturb him on the free sites. Nita finally gets him to go and have a look at the website from which Babli sent him her card: www.jacquielawson.com. That site takes no advertising but raises revenue through a low flat-rate annual or biannual membership fee:

> This site is funded by membership fees only and is an advertisement-free zone! No pop-ups, no spam, just great e-cards! We also have a really strict privacy policy so you can be sure that your details are safe with us. (jacquielawson.com 2005)

At the time of writing, the charge is £4.50 for one year, £8.00 for two (US$8.00/ US$14.00 or 7 euro/13 euro). In return for this not only do you get

those freedoms, you also get a choice of subtle, complex animated artwork by a
fine artist. The site is discreet and calm and does not overload. Best of all, from
Kumar's point of view, you can send as many cards as you like for more than two
years ahead. Kumar decides he can afford £8 and joins for two years.

As well as alerting him to the cash-raising hidden agenda, these experiences
also raise Kumar's awareness of those little boxes to tick or untick which can
expose you to tides of emails if you don't pay attention to them. He learns that it
is always a good idea to notice these and deal with them so as to make sure any
mechanisms for deluging you with unwanted information are switched off.
He knows he doesn't want any emails telling him how to spend his money,
trying to persuade him to buy this or that, trying to make him want things he
doesn't want.

While Kumar has been having the learning experiences just described, he
has been missing out completely on assignments for his maths A-level, though
he has just about kept up with the computing. One of the lessons Kumar has
learned is that he would very much like to access more money. He realises that
the business of having one's labours valued by society is the key to this for most
people. At more than twenty years of age it begins to dawn on him that he's
going to be poor for a long time if he is really going to go through university
(getting A-levels first) before being able to earn a living. He doesn't like this idea
at all and is tempted immediately to give up *both* his A-levels. After some
argument with his father, Kumar officially gives up the maths but agrees to press
on with the computing.

Through his local Connexions adviser, Kumar is told about his right to
further non-university education via the Learning and Skills Council (LSC). On
the website, www.lsc.gov.uk, he spots the apprenticeship list, encounters the
wide-eyed girl exclaiming with excitement about being able to earn and learn at
the same time, and he becomes excited too. When he explores the apprenticeship list Kumar's interest in metal work is revived: he doesn't have to learn in
college after all, he may be able to get an apprenticeship in this. Two possibilities
beckon him from that list, one the possibility of jewellery making, the other the
possibility of becoming a laboratory metallurgist. Now the videos they have
shot of Kumar experimenting with metal prove really useful. He sends a CD
with those on to the Connexions adviser with a covering letter drafted with help
from Nita, written on his laptop and printed out on good paper.

Meanwhile, Kumar continues developing his relationship with Irene.
Thanks to his online connections, he has finally reached a point at which he can
accept that he fits the diagnosis he's been given. Since he was told about his
diagnosis at the age of 16 he has been resistant to the idea of it: his self-image is
crucially that of someone who gets things right; someone who is personally all

right. The idea that he is someone with a disability is an idea Kumar used to dislike very much; his visits to www.neurodiversity.com make a huge contribution towards changing that. Now he thinks of himself as someone who has been enabled as much as disabled by his differences from other people. Along with his growing self-acceptance as an 'Aspie', and his growing knowledge of Irene, some of the links he follows up from the neurodiversity site turn Kumar into an iconoclast. He becomes, 'One who attacks and seeks to overthrow traditional or popular ideas or institutions'. He becomes a crusader for a different view of autism.

Kumar downloads the whole of *Getting the Truth Out* onto his laptop in order to show it to Irene and any of her support workers who are willing to take the time. He goes round there with this in mind, and happily catches Anna on duty. Anna is pleased to see him too, since she has come to realise that he knows much more about PowerPoint than she does. As a junior manager, part of her job is to deal with training issues. Too many of the staff are still frightened of using the computers, and senior management is concerned that their expensive invest-ment in IT is not paying off. Anna has learned quite a bit from Kumar and knows that he has always been able to answer all her questions about what to do in PowerPoint. He is not diffident about this. She has been wondering how Kumar would cope with explaining some basics to staff about using computers so that they can better support Irene and other residents. Anna asks Kumar what he thinks about this; he is absolutely delighted. This is the first time in his adult life that anyone in the material world as distinct from the e-world has truly appreciated what he has to offer – members of his family oscillate between doting and despair. To Kumar, this feels like the first time that he has been treated as a real member of society in the world beyond his family. He accepts with alacrity.

Kumar has also got reasons for feeling pleased to see Anna. He has realised that the quest to find Irene's family won't get anywhere unless he is able to find out more from her files. Anna explains to him that unfortunately the rules around confidentiality and her personal work obligations mean that she cannot just go to the files and find out Irene's mother's maiden name and tell him it, nor the address where she grew up, nor the schools she went to. All Kumar knows is Irene's surname (presumably based on her father's), the fact that she had brothers and sisters, and the fact that she had moved from her home to the insti-tution at the age of seven. This is not enough information for further investiga-tion to be possible. The rules mean Anna has to get permission from her line manager before she can tell Kumar anything from the files. However, she does know that Irene has always lived in this part of town, and that some of the elderly parents who run the Gateway club/disco she attends most weeks may know more. So she tips Kumar off and he arranges to go along with Irene to her next Gateway visit. Meanwhile, Anna will propose to the management that Kumar should be allowed to know some basic facts about Irene so long as Irene does not object. She will also propose that he should be offered some money for doing the training he has offered to do for nothing.

Today Anna and a couple of other members of staff who are on duty are urged by Kumar to sit down with him and Irene and watch the *Getting The Truth Out* show. Of course they have too much to do to spend that amount of time. But they do start watching and he does get one of them far enough to see the value of a communication board to the website's author. Irene sits right through, looking with interest. Kumar reads out some of it, but reckons that there's more text than Irene can cope with so he skips lots. He transfers a copy of the show to Irene's computer hoping she might browse at it without him.

Overall, Kumar is very pleased with the outcome of this visit to Irene's home. Irene has shown an interest in having a communication board and generally a more persistent interest in *Getting the Truth Out* than he had expected. He has a date to see her again, he has some definite steps which he can take to pursue his quest, and he has been asked to do something that he feels confident he can do well. He gets home and rings Nita up in excitement to tell her he has been asked to do the training, Kumar is completely surprised when she asks him how much he is being paid for doing this. Even though he has been worrying about money and how to earn it, it has not occurred to him that he might be paid for doing this work which he has so willingly volunteered to do. Kumar does not know what to do about this, but is hugely relieved when Anna rings a couple of days later to say she can offer him £70 for the training session. He'd been feeling he could not raise the matter himself and had been kicking himself for not having thought of being paid for the work. This reminds him that another apprenticeship offered on the LSC website he might be looking into is in Information Technology (IT). It is only much later on that Kumar discovers what a bargain he had been, doing a training session for so little.

When Kumar and Irene meet at the Gateway Club, her support worker introduces him to the old stalwarts who've been running the club long enough to have middle-aged children coming along with them. He is introduced as Irene's 'advocate' and he is greeted warmly. He immediately announces his quest, telling them that he wants to help Irene find her family using genesreunited.com. This, which is intended as explanation, causes some confusion because his listeners have never used the Internet, and they don't know anything about 'jeans reunited' and have no idea what Friends Reunited refers to either. Kumar becomes rather flustered by this failure to understand him but luckily a tactful soul breaks in to suggest a cup of tea, and the bad moment passes without getting any worse.

While he is having his tea one of the parents, John, comes over to chat with him. He tells Kumar that he used to know Irene's family because Irene and his son Pete had been in the longstay hospital together. John and his wife used to organise bus outings for the children a few times each year, to the zoo or the seaside. One of Irene's sisters, June, had been attracted to Pete's brother Ant on one of these outings and it had turned into a long-term relationship. Then she'd gone and run off with a chap called Purkiss and broken Ant's heart. Ant might be able to remember more. John offers to talk to Ant, and Kumar enthusiastically agrees to come back next week to hear more. Irene is not part of this discussion, but she appears happy throughout. It is hard to tell how much she may have followed of what they were saying.

Meanwhile, having dropped his maths A-level, Kumar is just about managing to meet his deadlines for his computer course – much cheered by his Jacquie Lawson cards regularly arriving to remind him. However, he has been much more keenly involved in creating a special programme for Irene than in doing his coursework. The 'reading with PowerPoint' programme Kumar is creating for Irene is going very well and is engrossing him, but it unfortunately cannot be used towards his computing A-level, because from the point of view of computer programmers, using PowerPoint hardly even counts as using a computer! He knows that connecting a sound to an image of the letter which represents it and stringing those separate sounds together to make familiar words seems an effective strategy. Kumar reckons that connection between sounds and meanings may be what Irene is missing. He thinks she seems to recognise individual words or groups of words on the computer screen as having meaning in that context – i.e. 'within the computer screen' in relation to events that occur in that space. But it is not so obvious that she associates them with any particular sounds – she may not realise their connections with the noises people make. The extreme inconsistencies of the relationship between the written and the spoken word in English make it particularly hard to recognise their connection anyway.

To make it interesting to Irene, Kumar decides to do spoken spellings of some of Irene's favourite places – the places she and Anna had been discovering together. He decides that since Irene has some familiarity with the Widgit Rebus symbols he will include these symbols of the objects whose names he is spelling out in the show. Kumar discovers the two ways of adding sounds into a PowerPoint show – through a narration (see Chapter 3) or through 'Insert' → 'Movies and Sounds' → 'Sounds' → 'Record' (Helpsheets A and B). He chooses the latter option because he wants the sounds to be triggered by actions Irene will hopefully take. Since Irene is now regularly going to church at St John's, and perhaps for nostalgic reasons, too, since it is where they first went together,

Kumar decides to target that as Irene's first spelled-out phrase: 'Saint John's Church'. He enters a large letter 'S' into his first slide, highlights it and presses 'Ctrl' and 'K' – the key strokes for turning it into a hyperlink (Helpsheets A and B). He makes the link within the document (i.e. the show he is making) and chooses 'Next' as the location to anchor to. He then creates a new slide (Ctrl+M), chooses 'Insert Sound', and 'Record' – Kumar's laptop has a built-in microphone; some might need to have a microphone plugged in to make adequate recordings. Anyway, he then records 'S…' so that it will come on automatically when the slide is visited (Helpsheets A and B).

On the next slide he writes '…ai…' and repeats the procedure, turning it into a hyperlink to the next slide, repeating the text in the same size and the same place, adding a recording of the sound which plays when the slide opens. Then '…n…', then '…t', and then he writes the whole word, hyperlinks that, and records 'Saint'. It's a slightly tedious procedure, but the end result is that if Irene clicks on the hyperlinks they will take her to the next slide that way or if she just hits the space bar to move the show on, the sound will play either way. Kumar builds up the names of half a dozen of Irene's favourite buildings this way. He also uses one of Irene's digitised photographs of each building, so that when, for example, the whole phrase 'Saint John's Church' is said, the picture of the church immediately pops up.

When he runs through the whole show Kumar is very pleased except for one thing. The carefully spelled pronunciation he has recorded doesn't match the actual sound people make when they casually say, e.g. 'St John's'. So he goes back and re-records the whole phrase 'St John's Church' in a version he labels 'casual version' in which the word 'Saint' gets its shorter, less articulated sound. Kumar shows what he has done to Anna and she suggests that as well as the photos, there could be links to the videos she and Irene made to show Irene's PCP meeting her newly developed interest. Kumar puts the show onto a CD and copies his show onto Irene's computer; with Irene's permission and her keen interest he then takes up Anna's suggestion and adds links to the video material of all Irene's favourite places. He makes this a two-way link so that Irene can go from the title page of each video to a matching spoken title, and vice versa.

Eight local places which Irene likes to visit have been assembled onto one page by one of the more technologically confident support workers. She has placed still pictures of each place side by side so that they can all be surveyed at once, and she has hyperlinked each one to its own video. Three days of each week throughout Irene's calendar have a link to this slide (Chapter 9). This is so that Irene can choose where she'd like to go on any particular occasion. Now when Irene chooses one of those she can choose to have its name said out loud too. Whether or not Kumar has succeeded in inspiring in Irene an under-standing of a connection between the spoken and written word, he has certainly given her something new to do which she appears to enjoy – and which impresses other people too. All this helps prepare Irene to use the communica-tions board which has been ordered, when it finally arrives.

Chapter 6

Living and Learning

Since talking to Jim at the Gateway Club, Kumar has been back to genesreunited.com, armed with enough information to start a family tree for Irene. He has the names of all her siblings; he has one sister's birth date; he has her mother's maiden name. This is enough to start a family tree online. When he's made it he shows it to Irene; he's not sure whether she understands what she's looking at – but she does look, and seems very interested, especially when she hears the names of her siblings. The information which is now online at genesreunited also makes it possible for other members of her family to get in touch with Irene via email. Irene gets an email account of her own. She uses a symbol-to-text (and vice versa) programme for this, the Inter_Comm symbolised email system from Widgit Software Ltd. This system uses photographs instead of names in its 'Address Book'. Kumar checks Irene's emails – with her permission, and demonstrating how he does this each time – whenever he visits. Three weeks later an email arrives in Irene's inbox to tell her to visit the Genes Reunited site, where a message awaits her. At this point, Kumar becomes very excited. There is a flurry of emails, and one Sunday afternoon two siblings, one sister-in-law and a nephew appear in Irene's life. Her brother becomes a fairly regular visitor, and she gets invited to his home, too. They meet Kumar as well and are enthusiastic about what he's done. It's an exciting time for the family to be re-connecting, just as Irene is beginning to be recognised as someone who may have real intelligence behind her over-whelming communication problems.

Irene's communication board has arrived. She can't easily comprehend what the options mean until she has experienced using the board. That means that without direct guidance from her, everyone who knows Irene has to imagine the situations and choices in which this board is going to be used. Obviously this is an occasion to build on what everyone knows about what Irene has chosen to do so far. A lot of discussion goes into what will be the important symbols for Irene. Kumar is involved in this process of identifying Irene's main interests, and the meeting does begin with Irene attending it too.

But after a very short time Irene gets up to leave, so any chance of involving her at this stage is ruled out. The good work support workers have been doing, especially since person-centred planning became obligatory, means that they have a very good idea about what Irene is likely to need. It is hoped that once Irene has got used to using it with staff and with Kumar that she will be able, for example, to tell people in cafés what she wants. Everybody who goes out with Irene is urged to ask her to use it to indicate her preferences at every available choice point.

The people working out what to programme into Irene's communication board include a 'something else' choice so as not to close off possibilities within this communication system. They include 'Yes please' and 'No thank you' buttons too. At the moment Irene can convey the yes/no meanings perfectly clearly to people who know her. Probably even strangers would find her standard 'no' gesture obviously meaningful – it's a fierce turning away of the head accompanied by a loud exclamation. But although the meaning is clear, the loud exclamation is socially catastrophic; everybody hopes Irene will soon be using this new way of saying no. Irene's way of saying yes, however, was not obvious to most people, though if they observed closely, when she reached up and touched the side of her nose they'd have seen that she looked pleased and excited when doing so. Another meaning, which Kumar insists should be included, is 'Please leave me alone'. They include a 'Thank you' button too, just in case.

The new communication board is programmed to say words out loud when certain keys are pressed. It is not a spelling device. Each key has either a symbol for a verb or other part of speech, or a small image of an object. It is not an instant success with Irene, but after a few weeks in which everyone very consistently encourages her to use it she begins to use it herself. They all encourage her to use it by waiting until she does so before taking the action she is choosing. Generally, staff had been in the habit of anticipating Irene, with their good knowledge and their confidence in understanding her needs and wants. This can create a kind of 'learned helplessness' which undermines learning how to act or even judge effectively by unthinkingly suppressing opportunity (see the website www.ldonline.org for some discussion and background about the idea of learned helplessness).

Because the communication board talks the same language as everybody else, it is a significantly more effective way to communicate with the world at large than hand signals or written symbols which are not part of the wider culture. Because it makes a noise, it can get attention. Its effect is quite a lot like Stephen Hawking's voice synthesiser, though it obviously has a much more restricted range. Because he is so famously a clever man, using one of these devices in the early twenty-first century has very positive social consequences. As you may have noted, they have programmed the device to speak very politely to add to the over-all good impression it creates.

A different sort of communication device is something Kumar first encounters in the *Ask and Tell* book (Shore 2005), namely a laminated card or list of vital information about autism, and about oneself, with phone numbers to ring in case of emergency. If something like this looks official, so much the better – it may have to persuade people in authority. Those people may have the authority to arrest one or decide one has a potentially dangerous mental health problem. One autistic man who uses such cards was visiting London (England) in August 2005. This man is very able to travel without support, so long as he has opportunities to prepare himself, and so long as he doesn't become overwhelmed by one of his sensory issues, or by toxic shock from food, or by social pressure. In any of these situations he is unable to speak and therefore unable to explain himself. During his four weeks in London, he was stopped by police six times. On five of those occasions his Autism Alert cards, which hang laminated from his belt, were able to communicate his needs effectively and prevent the situation worsening through ignorance, in spite of the fact that his ability to speak had evaporated each time. On the sixth occasion, the officer ignored the message on the card about involuntary reactions to a light touch, and it was fortunate the situation deteriorated no further. Kumar hears this story in his discussion group, and it sets him thinking.

Many autistic people can testify to the disasters which may follow from a public meltdown because of communication difficulties. After a successful pilot study the National Autistic Society (NAS) in the UK has produced an official-looking Autism Alert card:

> The Autism Alert card is designed to tell people with whom adults with autism come into contact about the condition, and asks them to show respect and tolerance. The card comprises a wallet which contains a leaflet of key facts about autism, and a credit-card style insert which can be used to include emergency contact details. (National Autistic Society 2005)

The information is available in 16 different languages to maximise its usefulness. It is part of a 2005 campaign by the NAS to raise autism awareness among the security forces. Maybe if the autistic man who was being hassled by the police for the sixth time had had an official-looking card like this, rather than his own home-made and rather well-worn laminated set, he might have been treated well by 100 per cent of the officers whose concern he aroused?

Kumar decides that both he and Irene could do with having one of the NAS cards. He has had a few occasions when he has been out and about on his own when he's had close encounters with 'the law'. Stories on his discussion group, which have emerged in response to the security forces issues being discussed, give him some clue about how dire the consequences could be. He does not want to spend the rest of his life being treated as a dangerous or challenging person, having his mind numbed by sedating medication and his human rights annihilated by the mental health system. He does not want to develop a tremor which means he needs a mouse like Irene's, specially designed to screen out the effects of shaking hands and fingers.

So Kumar gets two Autism Alert cards, one for himself and the other for Irene; the one for himself with details of Asperger syndrome and the one for Irene with information about autism as such. Like the diagnostic crtiteria themselves, there is a big overlap in the information about autism and Asperger syndrome. The information which comes with the card bluntly states that autism includes Asperger syndrome. Something Kumar has realised more and more as he has got to know Irene better is how similar he and she are. He knows she has lots of sensory issues too, which partly overlap with his. The other area in which it is fairly obvious that their dispositions overlap is the tendency to become very tense and anxious. What is more, the fact that they are very wound up a great deal of the time and finding it very hard to cope means that they are both likely to do things which bother other people. There is some online discussion of those issues, following from the stories about the occasions when it all goes wrong, which first put Kumar on to the NAS's Autism Alert cards. Lots of people report that they find it very helpful for their anxiety levels to have a long energetic walk, a run, a swim, trampoline, dance, cycling – any form of taxing exercise which builds endorphins and imposes minimal cognitive load. This is a recognised need in Irene's case, and an hour-long daily walk for her is already scheduled, though staffing issues often prevent it from happening. Kumar himself resolves to walk much more.

As well as those time-consuming and physically demanding ways of relaxing, a couple of people who were at the first Autscape conference in the UK report on some pleasing software – Reactive Colours[1] – which was being piloted there. Autscape, inspired by Autreat in the US which has been running for several years, is a conference-cum-retreat for people on the autism spectrum. It is planned and run to reduce autistic stresses to a minimum. As the Reactive Colours website puts it, the programme 'provides an engaging, accessible computer environment for spontaneous imaginative play and lear- ning, in which even the most anxious autistic individuals may relax and

---

1   Dinah Murray has advised the Reactive Colours project since its inception.

communicate' (reactivecolours.org 2005). This software is freely available to download from www.reactivecolours.org and has open source code – that is, it is created with code available to the public. The open source code means that anybody anywhere with access to it can manipulate the output: the programmers have worked very hard to make it easy to use and to choose, for example, colours and sounds. It is designed to reward any exploration. At the same time as being enjoyable it also develops an understanding of cause and effect in people who use it, and gives opportunities to develop mouse and keyboard skills. People of all ages find it fun to play with, and they enjoy watching other people having fun with it. Autistic people often have a hard time finding things to do which seem fun to them and don't annoy other people. That means anything which combines autistic fun with social acceptability is particularly rare and valuable. Kumar goes to the website and downloads a few of the 'reactivities' he finds there. He finds that playing around with them and noting the way the colours and sounds react to what he does is an extremely agreeable recreation. It even makes him laugh out loud quite often. Nita likes watching him amusing himself in this way; she notes that he seems to get some of the satisfaction from this that he gets from affecting materials as in metal work, but without the sense that there is some goal he is driven to reach – and without the threat that something may go wrong. So he is very much more relaxed than he normally is when engaged in an activity. Kumar joins the Reactive Colours community so that he can contribute his ideas to the development of the software. He is convinced that Irene will find this a soothing pastime too.

Next time Kumar visits Irene he takes the time to download some reactivities from the Reactive Colours website onto her PC. He spends a while playing with those on Irene's system and she watches with great interest. His intuition is right that this will appeal to her as much as it does to him. He backs off and leaves Irene to explore Reactive Colours in her own time, and within a minute or so that's what she's doing. From that time on, Irene is nearly as likely to click on her Reactive Colours icon as she is to open her calendar for the day. There is a feature of the software which Kumar realises could be a way of working at Irene's keyboard issues: it is possible to set the programme to be controlled through either keyboard or mouse. With a lot of trepidation, Kumar decides to try using this feature as a way of luring Irene into using the computer keyboard. She is using her communication board when she's out and about now, and even when she's indoors, so she has acquired keyboard experience – but not on the computer itself. Kumar switches the setting from mouse activated to keyboard activated on his own machine first and shows Irene how it works (very simply) to do the same activities which she's been enjoying when using her mouse. Rather to his surprise Irene seems to find it particularly entertaining to be using the keyboard and not the mouse; she appears delighted to be creating the familiar effects in a new way. Everyone is encouraged by this relaxed attitude to the keyboard. They also note that Irene is getting used to making choices with the speech sounds speaking out the names of places she likes – this happens both with the communication board and on her computer, thanks to the PowerPoint show Kumar made.

It is decided to install a 'text-to-speech' (TTS) programme on Irene's computer – a wide variety of these is available.

> A user can type and simultaneously listen to the words they are typing. Though this can be distracting in the beginning, with repeated use the distraction become less intrusive. Words mistyped or misspelled are immediately recognized and can be corrected (a spell checker should be used along with TTS). TTS and word prediction programs are often combined to aid in writing. (snow.utoronto.ca 2005 – a very useful site for advice about adaptive technology, as is www.abilitynet.org.uk)

The website: www.laits.utexas.edu has a large number of free downloads (some trial versions, some complete) which are available in a wide variety of languages (Kumar is delighted to discover it includes Hindi). programmes of this sort can be set to read out every word; in many cases you can choose the speaker's gender and in some cases you can choose the speed and pitch at which the text will be spoken. Originally evolved for people with visual challenges, the software will also read out whole books – many of which can also be downloaded free. Marie, whose eyesight has been failing more and more, also benefits from having TTS software on her computer. Unlike Irene, Marie makes use of the books; she used to read lots of novels and has been minding very much that she no longer can. She uses Google to find a number of sites that offer free novels. Further investigation teaches her to look out for and avoid the constantly growing number of opportunities to read unpublishable or 'self-published' novels. Although some of them may be really good, what Marie wants now is to re-read old favourites and maybe explore some other work of which she has heard but which she has not read. Her short-term memory may be failing, but she knows her culture and enjoys knowing it. The Gutenberg project (www.promo.net/pg/) is her favourite website – even better than flickr.com – there, a huge number of books can be downloaded for free. The downside of using the TTS software for the purpose of reading out literature is that it is (at the time of writing) very insensitive to meaning and context and so mis-speaks rather often (for example, not distinguishing the meanings of 'lead' as a verb and 'lead', the noun) and has monotonous intonation. These features really bother some people, but Marie finds the mistakes quite amusing, and likes not having actorish characters taking over the meanings in the text.

Of course Marie is known to be thoroughly literate, while Irene is assumed by almost everyone to be completely illiterate. For Irene, Kumar finds a free download which reads out each letter phonetically as it is struck – just the effect he'd wanted to create using PowerPoint. He seeks a helpful site for tips about using TTS for encouraging people to learn to read and finds lots of Google hits – but as far as he can see they are all for children. For example, www.partnershipforlearning.org/article.asp?ArticleID=888 has good advice, and some fun links to interactive online reading – for children. Kumar thinks Irene might find those fun, and is sitting beside her showing her one of them when a member of staff firmly tells him that Irene is an adult and that it is important for her to have 'age appropriate' activities. This is a new idea to Kumar, and he finds it rather surprising since he has noticed members of staff have teddy bear key rings, Mickey Mouse watches, Snoopy badges, short white socks, and so on. However, it is clear to him that he'll get into trouble if he ignores this restriction, so Kumar does not try out the children's sites again. Mainly the staff are very keen on him, welcome him enthusiastically, and see him as a computer expert in a way he finds very gratifying. Kumar has big problems with criticism and he never entirely recovers his relaxed attitude towards the two particular staff members who 'caught him out'. It's lucky that Reactive Colours is aimed at adults as well as children.

Irene appears to like having words coming out on both her computer and her communication board, and crucially, she likes controlling what those sounds are. She has finally found an effective, credible and intelligible way of communicating. But it could get better. If she will make that leap to spelling out words herself she will be able to tell anyone anything – just as everybody else can. At the moment she is restricted to the pre-programmed choices; there is no chance whatever that she is going to start talking – but there's no good reason why she shouldn't write with a keyboard. Kumar is right to think that as far as 'age appropriateness' goes, being able to communicate is far more like being a real adult person than not being able to communicate is. Appearances are not all.

Using the keyboard for the Reactive Colours experience, although a breakthrough, is still not getting Irene involved in hitting specific keys on her computer keyboard. Among the staff, even Anna is not all that encouraging to Kumar's project to get Irene writing. They all say that they think that it's a good idea in principle, but it seems that they don't believe it in practice and don't want to spend any time working towards something which is so unlikely to happen. Kumar decides to conduct a little experiment. He looks at Irene's choosing page and copies the words used to describe the pictures, e.g. 'St John's

Church' into a series of new slides, each linked to the original. Each slide has one description in the same words and font style as in the original, but larger and in a different colour, and their order does not reflect the original order on her choosing page. He then sets the slides to be viewed in 'Slide Sorter' mode, in which each slide appears as a 'thumbnail' side by side with all the other slides. When they are displayed like this, choosing among them will use mouse movements closely equivalent to those she already uses to make choices. So, staff – however sceptical – agree to offer Irene her choices of where to go using just the words, unless she finds that upsetting.

It is explained to Irene that this new display with just words is her choice page for now, and it does not seem to slow her down or inhibit her at all. Irene rolls the cursor immediately onto one of the slides and clicks there – it links her through to her usual choice page with every choice displayed and illustrated. The question is, will Irene click on the picture which matches the words she would have clicked on when there was no picture to guide her choice? And the answer is, yes! She repeats the verbal choice with her picture choice every time. It is persuasive evidence that she can at least recognise some words as being attached to meanings. After this, the staff become much more enthusiastic about the idea of encouraging Irene to write.

One member of staff, Dawn, has an idea about getting Irene writing which had not occurred to Kumar. She and he agree that Irene is not making a mental connection yet to the physical business of using the keyboard one key at a time. Irene needs to take the final step and hit specific keys to make the letters appear. Irene learned to use the mouse with a firm hand held over hers, wheeling it round and watching the cursor trail, seeing its effect in specific places, and feeling the click when the hand pressed down on it. Dawn suggests that people could facilitate Irene taking that next crucial step if they used the same technique, of manually guiding Irene's hand to spell out words she likes. Because she and Anna are aware of rules about touch and restraint which might make problems for Kumar if he takes hold of Irene's hand in the way required, they bring the family into this discussion. Happily they all agree, and Irene herself does not object, so long as the hand which is guiding hers is not light and tickly – both she and Kumar find that a touch like that evokes a startle response. So, Kumar goes ahead, using the text-to-speech programme while he guides Irene's right-hand index finger from key to key. Irene does not resist this guidance – but also does not start to take the lead until they have had a few sessions. Just as they have with Marie and with Kumar, emails turn out to be a great way to motivate Irene at the keyboard. Ever since the first email from her brother, thanks to Genes Reunited, she has appeared to enjoy messages appearing in her inbox. Now Irene starts to send short answers – the necessary breakthrough has happened!

In *Ask and Tell*, Shore (2005) makes the point that one of the best ways of getting messages across is on a T-shirt. A couple of the T-shirts worn by the central character in *Getting the Truth Out* strike Kumar as very suitable for Irene. One says, 'Not being able to speak is not the same as not having anything to say', which is a quote from Rosemary Crossley of facilitated communication (FC) fame. The other T-shirt he likes says, 'You do not know what I see, what I believe, what I dream, what I know. You do not live my life. You cannot be my voice'. The back of the T-shirt says, 'To be nobody but yourself in a world that is doing its best to make you everyone else is to fight the hardest battle that anyone can fight – e.e. cummings'. It is from a website called www.thenthdegree.com. The hand-over-hand approach which Kumar has eventually taken to connect Irene with the keyboard, is close to the procedure used in FC for the same purpose. Originally developed for use with people who have cerebral palsy and have difficulty in making accurate movements, it was felt FC could help people on the autism spectrum, too, since they often have movement issues as well as communication issues. It's a controversial approach mainly because in some cases messages were demonstrably coming from the 'facilitator' whose hand was controlling the keyboard action rather than facilitating it. Recent technological developments have made it possible to show that in many cases the person whose finger hits the keys really is in control. Andy Grayson's work with a group of non-speaking adults with autism has now demonstrated beyond any doubt that their able deployment of vocabulary at the keyboard is genuinely their own (Grayson 2004). Unfortunately unless the facilitation is faded out fairly rapidly – as was the case with Irene – a permanent dependency on having a facilitator present may easily develop.

They can't find a pre-printed T-shirt on sale with the 'Not being able to speak is not the same as not having anything to say' statement. So Kumar and Irene decide to make some themselves. Kumar visits a computer store and comes back with a packet of A4 iron-on transfers. You make any old design you want and print it out in the usual way onto one of these specially prepared sheets. You then follow the instructions for that particular kit – usually involving a protracted period of applying a very hot iron. To create their T-shirt messages – there were several iron-on transfers in the pack – Kumar and Irene use PowerPoint yet again, because it's so easy to use and because Irene is familiar with it already.

First Irene and Kumar open the 'File' menu in a new PowerPoint show and select 'Page Set-up'. They then choose 'Slide' and switch it from its default 'Landscape' setting to a 'Portrait' orientation – i.e. they switch it from horizontal to vertical. To get the message across visibly the vertical orientation will fit the bill much better, ensuring all the words are easy for people to read. For the same reason it's important to have a good strong contrast between background and foreground. They could just stick to big black letters on a white background for maximum legibility – but that is also banal and therefore not eye-catching as required. Kumar asks Irene if she likes the 'graffiti look' which has been used on the home page of *Getting the Truth Out*, and she does. So they do their best to mimic that, though they do not want to use just black and white.

The first thing they do is go to Google Images and put in the phrase 'brick wall'; several images are of plain brick walls, flat on which will make a good background. They download the ones which seem most promising. Next they choose 'Slide Background' from the 'Format' dropdown menu (Helpsheet B), there they go to the bar underneath the 'Background Fill' window and click on that – this gives them more options, labelled as 'Fill Effects'. They choose 'Picture' and enter a brick wall. They experiment a bit and discover that ones with sharp detail and contrasting bricks and mortar do not show up their message well; they find one which strikes them as just right and choose that for the background. Now they find that their choice of font looks rather stiff and unconvincing as graffiti. So, back to Google, they put in the phrase 'graffiti font' and find this website: www.graffitifonts.com/fonts.shtml. Here there is a long list of free graffiti style fonts to download. This is a very simple process. Once you have restarted your computer any fonts you have downloaded will automatically appear in your font list whatever programme you're using. Until you restart you won't be able to use them – this is no different from most downloads, which standardly require a restart. So they download two or three of the nice scrawly informal graffiti fonts, restart the computer, and choose one of them to make the message look handwritten.

For his own T-shirt:

> THEY WANT
> YOU TO
> PRETEND
> TO BE
> NORMAL...

on the front, and

> JUST SAY
> NO!!!

on the back is Kumar's first choice, for which he thinks a polite Times New Roman font will be just right. He wants to incorporate a bell curve into the graphic – that is one of those graphs which show distribution of traits of some sort. They always have an area in which most of any given sample is found, and a bell-shaped curve is used to represent a normal or statistically probable distribution. He finds a nice image of this curve with Google Image Search (Helpsheet D) again, and arranges it all using PowerPoint. In spite of his computing A-level Kumar does not just choose to use PowerPoint to please Irene – he goes on finding it beautifully easy to use. In fact, since giving his very successful talk to the staff about using the programme, Kumar has become even more of a PowerPoint enthusiast. He loves the fact that everybody, including himself, finds it so easy. He also likes being known as an expert!

Kumar and Irene now both go around sometimes wearing their assertive T-shirts. The ability to print anything of one's choice to a high quality and/or in large quantity is a great feature of computers, which also allows Kumar to make himself some smart business cards using PowerPoint and importing his own photograph.

Blogging...

When she was young, until her mid-20s, when she began having children, Marie used to keep a rather detailed diary. Her involvement with the local history group has got her re-reading her diaries, since the usefulness of that sort of account of daily life is much discussed at the group meetings. She is asked to prepare another talk based on those early diaries and she is having a fun time putting together reminiscences combining her old photos with anecdotes from the diaries. She will make it into a PowerPoint show and have it projected during her talk – just the purpose for which the programme was originally designed.

Now that she has a calendar on her computer (Chapter 9) which she looks at every day, Marie has decided to go back to regularly writing down the main events of her day. She is becoming frustrated by how blank her memories of recent events become without prompting, so she decides to help matters along in this way. With a bit of help, Marie's mobile phone is programmed with a reminder for her to go and do this at about 9 pm each evening. At that point, she looks at her calendar to remind her of what has happened, and that jogs her memory. Marie knows how to add a linked slide (a hyperlink) to each day, on which she makes a record of that day.

As well as recording any events which have happened in the world, such as visits she has made or received, and places to which she has been, Marie also likes to make a record of her visits to flickr.com and the pictures she has admired or shared there. Again, her memory is easily prompted by her browser history – Flickr is the only site Marie visits at all often apart from the Gutenberg Project and her knitting discussion group page. Any emails she's had from family or from her new friends are equally retrievable each day, and she likes to record those too in her daily log. So Marie takes to spending upward of half an hour a day creating this record.

On one of her visits to flickr.com, Marie notices the word 'blog' on the screen – and is puzzled by it. She asks one of the staff what it means, but the staff member doesn't know either. Marie forgets about it, but the staff member asks her computer literate family for help and explains the next day what a blog is, namely a sort of online public diary. The word is short for web log, and it turns out that there are lots of ways of making your own blog at no cost. All someone has to do is register on one of the sites such as Blogger, Xanga and Blogstream, choose a name for their blog, and they can start posting a record of their life for public reading – and comment. You might wonder why anyone would want to do that, and the reasons vary hugely. These days whole corporations have their own 'blogs'. A history of the development of these new entities which began to spring up just before the new millennium can be found online via the website www.rebeccablood.net.

Anyway, Marie can see a reason for having a blog: since discovering email and its easy potential for distribution she has been very tempted to copy every message to and from every other family member to every other family member, so that everyone would hear from her pretty much every day. But, as we've said, Marie is very socially graceful, and she realises that people who get a lot of emails may feel rather overwhelmed by them, and may even feel oppressed by an obligation to reply. She has resisted the appeal of what would in effect have been an email circular because she is concerned not to become tiresome. Creating a blog is a really neat way round this. Only the family members who care enough and have the time will log in, the ones that are usually too busy can catch up from time to time. But the ones who don't care enough to do that at this point in their lives won't be under any pressure to keep up with their cousin/granny/great aunt at all. It seems to Marie to be a perfect solution, and from now on she copies the daily log which she's been writing for her own benefit into a blog page hosted by Flickr. When it suits, she can include pictures which she's been sent – usually of how the youngest generation is coming along. Usually she just copies her log page and pastes it into the blog.

Something surprisingly similar has happened to Irene. For at least the last decade the events in Irene's life have been chronicled daily in the log book which records everyone's activities in her residential home. These logs are kept in countless homes up and down the country to meet a legal obligation to keep such records. The people they are about hardly ever write a word about themselves – probably in most cases they don't even know what's been written about them. If someone tries to go into the office and read their own log they are likely to be intercepted and turned back without anyone discovering their purpose. The logs are written by support workers at the end of every shift and are read by other support workers but otherwise treated as confidential – visitors, even family members, do not usually get to see them. They are, however, sampled by people who are monitoring service provision, as a way of finding out how good a service is being provided and how well individual service users are having their needs met.

In the light of Valuing People (Department of Health 2001) and its call to treat people with learning disabilities as real people, Anna decides the process of log keeping is going to have to be transformed. She tells all the staff that the log is to be kept in a digital form from now on, and is going to be accessible for each service user within their personal Desktop set-up. Service users are to be involved in the process, and Widgit Rebus symbols are to be used where necessary to ensure that the subjects of these logs can access their meanings as texts. Wherever possible, service users should write their own logs. What is more, after extensive discussion, it is decided that if the service users are happy to share their logs with other people, that will be fine. A bonus for management is that digitising the log-keeping process gives them an opportunity to gather some standardised data alongside the logs. They get their software expert at headquarters to create a short series of tick boxes which can be individualised to reflect people's personal goals, e.g. Did X go out today? Did X get to choose where to go? Did X go where X chose to go? Once the system is in place it will be possible to monitor service provision to all the service users using the system by compiling results from the tick boxes. Anna's idea for empowering the service users has all-round benefits.

Chapter 7

Getting Together

Taking Part in Meetings

It is the centenary celebration of St John's Church, and both Irene and Marie get asked to take part. The celebration has events inside and outside the church, and is very well attended after an article in the local paper. One of the congregation has been at one of Marie's local history society talks and knows that she was married in the church and had all her children christened there. Marie's photos and her reminiscences are made into a PowerPoint show which is set to play continuously and is projected brightly in a dark corner of the church. Irene, who has been going to the church service, has also contributed the digital video she and Anna made of St John's Church itself. Kumar has lent his laptop for the occasion so this is playing too, on the table next to the projector. Anna is there to support Irene, and she recognises Marie as one of her company's service users! She introduces Irene, Kumar and Marie to each other.

Not long after that, our three heroes, having now all met each other, are given the opportunity of becoming members of the same group. A consortium of Housing Associations invited adults with learning disabilities to be members of an Advisory Group. The Housing Association Consortium had already set up a Management Board which was to have representation from people with learning disabilities who were also tenants. However, at the first meeting of the Management Board some of the members suggested that it would be impossible for one or two tenants to be properly involved in the meetings alongside so many 'professionals' using jargon and in a hurry to complete the business parts of the meetings. They also argued that the tenants would not be representing the views of all tenants but only their own views and therefore it would be better to have more tenants involved in some way. Having been involved in a similar situation before, one of the Board members suggested having an Advisory Group whose membership would be people with learning disabilities (tenants) and chaired and facilitated by a member of the Management Board. This Advisory Group would meet approximately two weeks before each Board meeting and their views would be reported back by the chair, thus maintaining a meaningful link between the two groups. Tom Brown, a manager within a care-providing organisation who has responsibility for several houses and is a member of the Management Board, offered to chair the Advisory Group.

The next step was to decide how to choose the members of the Advisory Group. It was felt that a membership of approximately five (plus the chair) would be optimal. This would allow for a range of members but not be logistically unwieldy. Also costs had to be taken into account. It would obviously be more costly to arrange meetings for people with learning disabilities who would need more support to attend meetings, greater support needs between meetings and may need special transport and facilities to attend meetings. However, all Board members agreed that in order to really involve those people most affected by the decisions made by the Board, adequate resources to support the process must be provided. Drawing on his previous experiences, Tom suggested that each tenant of the housing consortium be sent information about the anticipated role of the Advisory Group in an accessible format, together with a nomination form. The same information was also sent to managers of the houses asking them to ensure that each tenant was given sufficient support to understand the information and the implications of being a member of the Advisory Group and to decide whether each tenant would like to nominate themselves or another person. A deadline was given for the return of the nomination forms.

Having sent out the information and forms, Tom had no idea how many people would be nominated but it was likely that the number would exceed the favoured number of five. This was, in fact, the case and there were eight nominees. Therefore, a vote would take place. It was suggested that all tenants be invited to attend a meeting where each nominee would give a short presentation about themselves and then a ballot would take place. This was an unrealistic expectation given the geographic spread of houses and the support needs of some tenants. Therefore an alternative was recommended. Each nominee was asked to put together a short biography. It was suggested that as most of the people who were voting were non-text readers the nominees should create their biography using PowerPoint. This enabled them to 'talk' about themselves and include photographs and video showing their likes and dislikes and to demonstrate their own personality. Each presentation was sent to Tom who then put them all onto a CD and circulated them to each house and tenants were supported to watch them and discuss any issues raised. Each tenant would be sent a voting form with the names of each of the eight nominees (with their photos) and they would vote for three people. The five nominees gaining the most votes would be the members of the Advisory Group. However, it was decided there would be a role for the three people not selected. They would each be invited to attend some meetings and would form a wider consultation group when it was appropriate to seek the views and opinions of a wider audience.

All three of our heroes received the information and decided that they would like to be members of the Advisory Group. Each felt that they had something specific to offer and that they would be able to represent their own views at the meetings and to advise the Management Board on many issues which would affect them personally. Each worked on a short PowerPoint presentation which they hoped would persuade others to vote for them. Having gathered many resources for their lifestories they already had a wealth of photos and short video clips to hand. However, it was difficult to decide which aspects of their lives they wanted to use in this presentation. So how did they each decide which information to tell and what they thought other people wanted to know about them to persuade them to vote for them?

It was difficult for Marie to focus on the here-and-now of her life and the skills that she has, with the exception of her knitting. However, she wanted to tell people that she had been a secretary and she thinks she will be able to use some of those skills, although they are, by her own admission, very 'rusty'. She thinks that she will be able to make sure that the room is ready for everyone when they arrive and will make sure that there are pens and paper on the table for meetings. So she has a slide about this in her PowerPoint presentation. She doesn't think that people will be that interested in her knitting patterns and photos of the things she has knitted but that they might like to know that she raises money for charity by selling her knitted dolls' clothes and that she sends many of her knitted baby clothes to children in 'poor' countries. She has letters from several charity workers thanking her for her kindness, so she is supported to scan a couple of letters and thank you cards and includes them in her presentation. Marie is also very proud of her home and the way she has her furniture arranged with lots of photos of her family prominently displayed. She wants a photo of her room in her presentation. These are the things which Marie thinks will make other people vote for her.

Kumar's choice of presentation is very different. He wants people to know about his ICT skills which have really progressed recently. He is more interested in showing people a very interactive presentation. His first page has his photo 'zooming in' and then filling the entire screen (Helpsheets A and B). He thinks this will create a real impact on the voters. He has seen a similar start to a party political broadcast and really liked it. Kumar wants people to know that he is studying for A-level. He is very proud of the fact that he has recently helped Irene to use the Internet and he wants people to know that he is a caring person.

He thinks that he will be able to help the Advisory Group by researching things on the Internet. He wants people to know that he is good at using the Internet so he includes a short video clip showing him looking up his local library. He is very pleased with the presentation and is sure that this will impress people and make them vote for him. When his final slide, which has a photo of him, is viewed, a message which Kumar recorded plays automatically asking people to vote for him. He thought about the last slide for some time and thinks this is the best way to finish as that is what they did on the party political broadcast!

It was more difficult for Irene's support worker to help her to create a presentation which shows her in a very positive light as someone who can represent herself on a committee such as the Advisory Group. However, she seemed to be keen to join her new friends and become a member of the group. But what can she offer and what will make people vote for her rather than the other nominees? Certainly showing her breaking glass will not impress anyone! However, Irene has many redeeming features. She likes to show visitors around the home, and there are always many people coming to look round, many of whom seem rather severe and do not take the time to tell Irene who they are or why they are there. Her supporter worker thinks that Irene will be able to make other members of the Advisory Group think about the behaviour of visitors to their homes and (with support) Irene will try to ensure that this is one of the items which the Advisory Group discusses. Therefore Irene's presentation does not say much about herself or her life but concentrates on the issues she wants the Advisory Group to discuss, mainly focusing on visitors. She thinks that the voters will all know how it feels when someone comes into their house without sending them a letter or telephoning first announcing their intended visit. And what happens when they do arrive, how does Irene know who they are? Irene wants everyone to send a photograph of themselves so that she can pin it up on her notice board enabling her to recognise visitors. Also she wants visitors to talk to her, not to the staff who happen to be on duty. After all it is her home.

Well, Tom did an excellent job of collecting all eight presentations and sending them to the tenants, with instructions to staff who may not be familiar with computers on how to access them. He even checked that all tenants had access to a computer and for those few that didn't he took around a laptop. Then the time came for voting for their three choices. As you would expect, our three immediately wanted to vote for themselves (which was allowed in the rules) and their two colleagues. It was difficult for the support staff to explain that they shouldn't vote for them just because they know them, but this is no different from any other voting system and in the end they couldn't be persuaded to do otherwise. They did look closely at the other presentations and they were encouraged to think about the things they liked about the person who was shown in the presentation and the things they were saying.

So how did our three get on? They were all successful and were voted as members of the Advisory Group. In addition to these three there were two clear winners. These were Lynn, a woman who has high support needs because of her physical disability as well as her learning disability. She finds speaking really difficult and it takes her quite some time to say just a short sentence. She is often very frustrated by people finishing her sentences for her or, even worse, speaking on her behalf. Lynn is in her mid-20s and has lived in a small residential home with four other people who are also wheelchair users. The home is very well adapted to their needs and affords them as much independence as possible. Lynn usually has two support workers with her when she leaves her home and she needs to travel in a specially adapted vehicle. This will pose many problems for our Advisory Group chair, Tom. There are many resource implications to consider when deciding on a meeting venue, such as access for wheelchair users, suitable toilet facilities, availability of staff and suitable transportation, suitability of the venue for those with sensory impairment (even though the Disability Discrimination Act of 1995 states that you must ensure your services are accessible to disabled people, accessibility still remains an issue for Lynn). In addition, meetings will have to be planned around Lynn's timetable as she has several sessions of physiotherapy each week and a hydrotherapy session which cannot be rescheduled.

Melanie is the fifth elected member of the Advisory Group. Melanie is considered to have severe learning disabilities. She has a very short attention span and although she enjoys new situations if she is accompanied by staff she trusts, she doesn't stay in one place for long and wants the freedom to wander away from the group. Melanie has a good sense of humour but imposes this on anyone around who has to listen to her repeated jokes time and time again. Melanie lives in the same street as Lynn and they have met on many occasions before.

The date for the first meeting was set. Tom decided to hold this in a meeting room at the day centre attended by both Lynn and Melanie. This would have the advantage of being accessible to Lynn and familiar surroundings for both Lynn and Melanie. He also anticipated that it would mean that there would be less difficulty in getting the level of required staff support and obviously would create no problem with transport, as Lynn would be scheduled to be at the day centre. The time and venue were convenient for Kumar, Irene and Marie. They were each supported by one person. Kumar's sister, Nita accompanied him but was determined that Kumar speak up for himself and not rely on her to speak out for him, building on the routine they had established prior to his care meetings. Irene and Marie were each accompanied by a support worker.

Prior to the meeting Tom had sent out an agenda. He wanted the meetings to be fairly informal, giving the members an opportunity to take the lead and feel free to speak out, but on the other hand he also wanted it to be run in a business-like manner with focused discussions. This made drawing up the first agenda extremely difficult as there would be so many things to cover and he had to decide on priorities. He timed the meeting to begin at 11 am. The first thing would be for people to introduce themselves to each other. He thought this would take some time considering the number of people attending, noting that the 'professionals' at the meeting outnumbered the Advisory Group members, a not unfamiliar situation for people with learning disabilities. Taking into account that Melanie would need some distraction and being unsure of the physical needs of Lynn and the other members, Tom decided on an early lunch. He thought this would be an enjoyable and social part of each meeting so he had carefully decided on a 'picnic' type of format. Having checked any special dietary needs of everyone attending, Tom had called into the local supermarket and bought fresh produce to give a variety to suit all tastes! He also bought drinks which would be available throughout the meeting. The group arrived on time and were directed to the meeting room. It was quite tense as it was a fairly large group of 13 people (five members, six supporters, an administrator to take notes and Tom), many of them not having met before. Tom welcomed everyone and offered them a drink. Then he asked them all to sit around the tables he had carefully arranged in a circle in the centre of the room. He had left a space for Lynn's wheelchair with easy access.

Tom started by introducing himself and he said that he would be leading the meetings and he would make sure everyone was allowed to speak when they wanted to, but there should be some rules to follow. (At a later stage in the life of the Advisory Group, Tom was to introduce a system of holding up coloured circles of paper, the colours denoting that someone wanted to speak or that they couldn't hear or understand what was being said.) Tom also said that it was fine if anyone wanted to leave the table and look at other things in the room. When it was Lynn's turn to introduce herself she struggled to get the words out and her support worker was about to finish the sentence for her, but Tom firmly but considerately stopped the support worker by saying that they had plenty of time and there was no rush for Lynn to finish. This helped to set the scene for the future for Lynn. As soon as Melanie had introduced herself and told two of her jokes she left the group saying she wanted to go to the toilet. As he suspected, the introductions took a long time and Tom smiled to himself as he pictured the contrast to the first Board meeting when introductions had been completed in no time at all!

Lunch worked well. Everyone enjoyed the relaxed atmosphere and the fact that they could choose their own food from a wide variety of things. Tom took the opportunity to observe what foods the Advisory Group members chose and whether anyone, particularly Lynn, had any difficulties in eating. He made mental notes for future meetings; he certainly wouldn't buy doughnuts again, as they were difficult to eat and left everyone's fingers sticky! Tom gave time for everyone to chat but not long enough for them to forget that the focus of the day was the meeting. The next item on the agenda was to talk about the sort of things they would discuss in future meetings. He asked people to think about this for the next meeting and then they would write down what issues people wanted to talk about and whether this was the role of the group. This was really the preparation for drawing up 'Terms of Reference' for the group. Tom also wanted people to think about where they would like to hold the meetings. To his surprise Lynn had very strong views on this. She said that she would like to go to different places for the meetings and not to have them in the day centre every time. Everyone else thought that this was a good idea too, but some of the staff were not convinced that it would be possible and cited the issues of staff time and transport, which Tom had known would be raised. Tom pointed out that they should work together within the ethos of a person-centred approach and overcome these obstacles. He said that he would arrange the next meeting at a different venue and if staff had problems with transport for Lynn he would see if he could help. In fact, Tom had anticipated this and had used the Internet to research the availability of a suitable vehicle for Lynn should her normal one be unavailable. He had found a local charity which would loan just such a vehicle for only £15 per day.

The last item on the agenda was communication. Tom wanted to talk about how he would send information to the group members. Most of them were used to information being directed through someone else. In future Tom would address information to the Advisory Group members and send a copy to their support person. The problem was how would members prefer the information to be presented? Tom had brought some examples with him. He had written the agenda in several different formats and showed them to the group. He was aware that the day centre where the meeting was being held uses symbols (Writing With Symbols 2000 from Widgit Software Ltd) but he had not been able to find out if any of this group uses symbols to support text. Then again there are several different symbol sets, such as PCS (Picture Communication Symbols from Mayer Johnson), or Makaton, or maybe the day centre had upgraded to the newest symbol list, Widgit Rebus which has lists in either black and white or colour. This would give several different options for producing the agenda but it became even more complicated when Tom thought about where the symbols could be placed. Individuals who have learned to read through symbol support may be used to seeing a symbol above (or below) every word. However, many people just need the keywords symbolised to remind them of the context of the text; in which case the symbols can be placed above or below the text. Alternatively, the agenda could be typed in a table in Word or in Communicate: In Print (a Desktop publishing application from Widgit Software which incorporates symbols) and symbols for key words placed in a cell alongside the text. Even this solution needs consideration. Many people put the symbols in a cell to the right of the text but there is an argument for putting pictures on the left, before the words, as this may make them seem more important. This is a good message to give out to people who may find written words hard to understand.

In all of the examples Tom had consistently used photographs whenever a person's name had appeared. He had inserted photos into a table at the beginning of the agenda to show who would be present. Tom has read many reports and articles on making information accessible, and although there are many viewpoints, all agree on how photos should be used to represent people. The photo should show just the head and shoulders of the person against a plain background. This may seem obvious but think about when you take a photograph. You know what the subject of the photo is but once the photo is developed and you show it to other people they may interpret the subject differently. Your photo of your mother with your daughter might appear to someone else as an old lady with a baby, to someone else as people feeding ducks and to yet someone else as an outing on a winter's day!

There are many other ways of making information accessible but Tom thought that this offered enough ways to act as a starting point for future discussions. He handed out the different formats and asked everyone to take them away and think about which they liked and they would all talk about it next time. Tom felt that it had been a good first meeting, but that he had done most of the talking, with the supporters also having lots to say. The people who should have spoken most actually contributed least. This wasn't an unexpected outcome, but one which Tom determined to change over time. He also knew that there was a great deal of work to do before the next meeting. First of all he had to send out the notes (minutes) of the meeting while it was still fresh in people's minds. He wanted it to be as accessible as possible to each of the members. He produced the notes in a Plain English (easy-to-read) version using short sentences with just one idea per sentence, jargon free. He knows that Kumar can read text but he isn't sure about the others. He then produced text supported by symbols in two different ways; first with the key symbols above the text and second with key symbols in to the left of the text (using a table in Word). He then recorded himself reading the text and sent it on a cassette to each Advisory Group member. Finally, he sent the notes on a CD to each Advisory Group member so that they could look at the notes on their computer and use a text reader, giving them more independence. Tom included instructions for staff telling them about text readers and how to download one free from the Internet (one example is from www.readplease.com, others have been mentioned in Chapter 6).

The next meeting was arranged for two months after the first and Tom sent out the agenda in advance (in the same formats as those in which the notes were sent out) making sure that it had photos on of all those invited to attend. The first item is always going to be a welcome to everyone. At the meeting Tom asked if the members had received the notes and the agenda and asked them which format they had preferred. Kumar lost no time in telling him that, although he liked having the photos to remind him of the names of all the people, he does not need or want the symbols. Irene had enjoyed listening to the cassette. However, when she was at the day-services she was able to see the notes with the photos and symbols and listen to the computer reading the text. She would like everything sent to her on cassette and on CD in future. Lynn, Marie and Melanie all liked the symbols support but were undecided about which symbols they liked and where the symbols should be placed. However, Melanie said that she didn't like the photo of her because she had changed her hairstyle since the last meeting and asked whether Tom would use a different one of her in future. Tom asked the other group members whether they liked their photos and Lynn said she would like one which didn't show too much of her wheelchair and she would like a prettier background. So the whole group moved into the garden to have new updated photos taken against a better background. As Tom used a digital camera he was able to take several photos and immediately download them onto the computer so that everyone could choose the one they wanted to represent them. Tom also learned from this, and at regular intervals he asked whether people were still happy with the current photos.

Over time Tom produced other examples of ways information had been presented in an attempt to make it accessible. He downloaded from the website www.publications.doh.gov.uk the report 'Nothing About Us Without Us' (the report to the government from the service users advisory group that helped write Valuing People) from the Valuing People website (www.valuingpeople.gov.uk). When he did this Tom made a mental note to show the Advisory Group this website at one of their future meetings as it has a bank of graphics which can be inserted into any document using 'drag and drop'. He also created a document using clipart he downloaded using Google Images to support the text. Tom gathered as much information as he could on making information accessible and he wasn't frightened to experiment with new ways. He realised that making information more accessible to the group is as much about the process as the end product.

There was great excitement and apprehension among the group when Tom told them that they had been invited to attend a joint meeting of the Advisory Group with the Management Board. The meeting would be held at the head office of the Housing Consortium and all ten Board members would be attending. Lynn did not hesitate in asking whether they could see around the offices and learn about the jobs people do there and Marie wanted to know if she could bring her current knitting project to show them. Kumar was more interested in whether they all have computers on their desks and what programmes they use. Irene worried that they wouldn't be able to have their lunch. This concern was shared by Melanie as both of them enjoyed the time they spent over lunch. Tom said he would ask all of these questions at the next Management Board meeting. He was determined that the meeting should be an enjoyable and memorable one for the Advisory Group members and that the Board members would learn some lessons too. Once the agenda for the meeting had been sent to him he translated it into accessible formats for the group.

Tom had gathered photos of everyone who would attend the meeting and organised these photos on a PowerPoint slide. He then created a slide for each person and alongside their photo he added a couple of photos which would help identify that person, such as the logo of the company they work for and a photo of the place they come from. (Tom didn't forget to put a button on the screen to take him back to the front slide.) He linked each of these slides to the front slide so that by clicking on the individual's photo he was taken through to the slide about them. Then he created slides for the short report Lynn wanted to read out to the whole group. Lynn was really worried that she wouldn't be allowed to read the report because she takes so long but Tom had said that this wasn't a problem (and he had already primed the Management Board members). Tom knew that some people would have difficulty in understanding Lynn so having the presentation on screen would help everyone, including Lynn.

The meeting was a great success. Tom set up the PowerPoint presentation using a data-projector before the meeting began. As each person introduced themselves, Tom clicked on their photo and the information about them was displayed. He repeated this throughout the meeting whenever anyone spoke or presented information. This acted as a reminder to the Advisory Group members (and several of the Board members admitted after the meeting that it had been useful to them too). In the debrief after the meeting the Advisory

Group members said that having the information about people highlighted made them feel less intimidated. Tom had organised their usual lunch and this familiar format also made them feel more relaxed. To Lynn the highlight of the day was being able to read out the report without being interrupted even though she had taken a long time. Kumar had been delighted to see that the office staff used the Internet and he was able to show a couple of people his favourite websites. Marie said that she had spoken with one lady who was a secretary like she had been so many years ago and this lady was interested in Marie's knitting as she has grandchildren and Marie is going to send her some patterns.

Tom was very keen to share the lessons learned working with the Advisory Group and he wanted the group to share in the dissemination of these findings, so, over several meetings, they wrote a report to be shared with the Management Board. First they looked at why they had enjoyed being part of the group. For Lynn this was easy; she had enjoyed visiting new venues and not being told that there was no transport available. She also valued being listened to and people taking time to let her speak for herself, even though she was very slow at getting her words out. Melanie liked the fact that Tom had bought her (as he had everyone else) an attractive folder to keep all the notes in. She was pleased that Tom had had the forethought to punch holes in all paperwork he had sent so that she could put them straight into her folder and not risk losing them while she waited for someone to find a hole punch. Melanie had even shown members of her family her folder and this had made her feel important. Everyone was surprised at how Melanie had, over time, become more involved in the meetings and had actually stayed throughout later meetings rather than wandering off. All of the group had enjoyed the lunches which Tom had provided and which had become so much part of the meetings as he had learned their favourite food items. They all said that they felt that their contributions had been valued by everyone in the group and that they had not been intimidated at the meeting with the Management Board because of the support they had been given.

Tom also wanted to reflect on how he had made information accessible and what this had meant to the group. The dictionary defines accessible as 'capable of being reached' and 'capable of being read with comprehension'. He concluded there were four steps to making writing accessible. The first was to decide on the key messages to that particular audience. He had to consider what the Advisory Group needed and wanted to know and also the level of comprehension of the targeted audience. This means that he automatically cuts out unnecessary detail.

The next step is to make the words and sentences easy to understand. This means cutting out all jargon, acronyms, abbreviations and any complicated words. Being direct also helps, so Tom uses words like 'I', 'we' and 'you'. He tries to make the text sound like speech, using positives and avoiding negatives which can be hard to understand. Having only one main idea in each sentence helps to keep sentences short and uncomplicated. Tom also includes direct quotes from the group members which will help them to recall discussions and ensure that their views are seen as important.

The third step is to consider the layout and design of the document. Tom uses a large font size (never less than 14 point) and a clear typeface. He found that the group really liked Comic Sans because the letter 'a' is written as people are taught to write it but Arial is an acceptable clear alternative. Tom has overcome critics who say he wastes paper because he leaves 'white space' in documents, as he can demonstrate that this makes documents less confusing. Tom never uses blocks of capital letters or italics as these make writing harder to read, but instead he uses bold to make headings stand out and short paragraphs to break up the text. He also ensures that he makes the text easier to read by not allowing a word to be split over two lines, and uses left justify rather than 'block' text (as seen in most printed books and magazines). In addition to these points, Tom ensures that the information given in the document is recorded in a logical, consistent manner.

The fourth step is the use Tom makes of photos, symbols and drawings to support text. Tom soon realised that there are many differing opinions of how useful these are and how to use them effectively. Through much discussion within the Advisory Group meetings he also realised that each of the members has different preferences too. There was no argument that images do support text and that they give clues to the content of the writing to people who are not confident readers. Photos of specific people and places can be very useful. Photos are not so good at communicating concepts as they often contain too much detail to convey a single concept. Symbols are used everywhere now and we are being exposed to them more and more but there needs to be more research to show which symbols are most helpful to people with learning disabilities.

For most people looking at a page full of symbols can be very confusing. Tom talks to support staff about this and to illustrate it he shows them a page of Russian text. He then shows them a page of symbols (from Writing With Symbols 2000) with the text hidden and asks them to 'read' the symbols. Tom encourages supporters to get to know the theories behind using symbols and to take time to learn the categories of symbols. He emphasises that using symbols will not automatically make the text comprehensible. Tom also warns staff that alternatives to symbols, such as drawings, often contain too much detail and confuse the message rather than clarify it. Most of all, Tom tells supporters, photos, symbols and drawings should not be included merely for decoration. They should serve a clear purpose, after all, graphics can make information easier to understand and remember. Some people will rely on graphics rather than text to make sense of a document.

Tom encourages people to think about making information accessible as without this the four key principles of the learning disabilities strategy Valuing People, namely rights, independence, choice and inclusion, are unlikely to be realised. Throughout the life of the Advisory Group Tom has consistently encouraged feedback and suggestions for improvement from the members on the way information is sent to them and he has learned from this and built on it, trying new ways of presenting information and abandoning those which were not popular. The biggest lesson Tom learned from this process is that making information accessible is extremely time-consuming, especially when the same information is to be presented in a variety of formats. Finding the right photo or symbols takes time, and setting up recording equipment and finding a quiet, uninterrupted few minutes is not easy! Documents with coloured photos and symbols are far more appealing and easier to understand than documents that have been photocopied so many times that they lose their clarity, but there is a cost implication. He is now negotiating with the Management Board to raise the budget for accessible information and facilitation of meetings for people with learning disabilities. The Board members are far more receptive having seen how empowered the Advisory Group were at the joint meeting and having read their report. We wish Tom luck and hope that he manages to get those additional resources!

Chapter 8

A Year or So Later...

A year or two later all three of our friends have moved on in various ways. Since the first Advisory Group meeting when Marie and Irene and Kumar all met properly for the first time, they have got to know each other quite well. Along with the other two voted to the group they meet once a month, and have a good meal together after dealing with issues on their agenda. (Irene and Kumar always make sure that they wear their declamatory T-shirts for these meetings.) They exchange emails, and Irene now sends and reads her own. They are treated with great respect by all the staff. They have been working with the management IT specialist to create a really accessible website, and a blog ring for all of Goodfolk's service users. Kumar has learned a great deal during this process, all of which makes him more employable and looks good on his CV along with his A grade for computing A-level.

Irene uses Communicate: Webwide (from Widgit Software Ltd) to explore the Internet because although she can read, tackling large amounts of text is extremely challenging for her. This programme allows her to format the text from any website into one column and to symbolise the text if she chooses. She can also select her own colour options for hyperlinks. The others only ever send her short simple clear emails. Sometimes Irene's emails are much longer than the brief manageable messages Marie and Kumar take care to send her. But she finds lots of websites overloading and is grateful for the simplifying translations Webwide provides. Irene's brother has her round once a week, after she has been to church, for Sunday lunch, often with other members of the family. Irene is no longer regarded as a difficult or unrewarding person with whom to work. People no longer talk down to Irene and assume that she is stupid. She used often to be unable to communicate because she was too upset and her distress was reliably treated as rage, or 'Irene having a tantrum'. Now she is much less likely to get that upset, though still sometimes much annoyed.

Irene now has a voiced communication board with a full keyboard similar to her computer's, into which she types when not at her main computer. It is a kind of large-scale PDA (personal digital assistant). That means that anything

Irene writes while out can be recorded and revisited later and/or downloaded onto her home system (it can be set to do this automatically). Some of its keys are also dedicated to produce whole phrases when activated. A terrific bonus is that the PDA even incorporates a satellite connection. That means that Irene can send and receive texts and emails while out and about, as most people with mobile phones now do. The PDA is set up so that with one press of one button Irene can call for support when needed. The satellite technology also means she can be quickly and accurately located on a map. Another wonder is that the PDA has a port for a webcam into which a little eye on a bendy neck is plugged – whenever it is activated it sends an audiovisual datastream up to the website which Kumar and the others on the Advisory Group have been working on. So when it's switched on everything that's happening around Irene is being recorded and transmitted.

Before she got this latest PDA Irene's carers naturally felt it would be irresponsible to let her go out on her own. They thought that at the very least someone should go with her and shadow her closely whenever she went out, which in turn meant that she got out far less than she wished to. When she did, it was observed that she was safe at crossing all the local roads, choosing always to use proper crossings – following years of good example from support staff. So now Irene sometimes goes out without a personal fleshly assistant because she can let her care providers know what's happening, and she can call for help effectively. Not only can she signal that she needs help, but she can be easily found by someone who knows her if she does. This has been discussed with Irene, since some staff suggest that it is intrusive to have this tracking device turned on. But Irene likes maps, likes the idea of being found on a map, and would find it more intrusive to have a member of staff still following her around as they used to. Irene gives her assent to the tracking. Being able to use the PDA to communicate in shops and cafés was a giant step towards independence, these extra features add an unanticipated degree of security.

Luckily, because it is not small and trendy, Irene's PDA is unlikely to be stolen. The same cannot be said for Kumar's PDA. Kumar wears his on a lanyard round his neck, and always hides it underneath his jacket. He uses it as an MP3 player too, and listens to music on it with earphones most of the time when he is out. His family has clubbed together to get him one with all the latest features. So like Irene's it has wireless Internet connectivity, satellite location software, and can also pick up and transmit a stream of audiovisual data. It also has a HELP button like Irene's so that if he gets into a crisis when he's out without support he can contact back-up. This has made it possible for Kumar to get out of a couple of crisis situations. His Autism Alert card and the detailed advice enclosed with it is a great help in most of his difficult encounters with the authorities. But every now and then Kumar has a problem with someone who does not take any notice of what it says on his card. At those moments, when he has been becoming more and more agitated, he has found the HELP button invaluable. Whoever responds to the call for help speaks to the problematic official and explains his issues and that his manner and behaviour may wrongly provoke suspicion.

Marie does not have a PDA of any kind. She finds her fairly basic mobile phone and her computer already tax to the full her willingness to learn new technology. What is more she is less and less inclined to go out because it is such an exhausting and often unrewarding business. But she does have a webcam in place at home and her main activity these days is writing a daily blog featured on the Goodfolk's dedicated blog ring, which is in effect a relatively private forum. Her reporting on her far-flung family is a highlight of these reports, which she intersperses with reminiscences about the world she grew up in and how it's changed. The daily record-keeping has had a very positive effect on her capacity to keep track of daily events and may even have improved her memory for recent events. At the same time as posting to the Goodfolk blog ring, she posts each message to a public blog hosted on www.flickr.com and has had some response from local history buffs as well as from members of her family. A CD of Marie's story made up of a radio interview with a local historian plus her own illustrated PowerPoint shows is proving a best seller for the local society.

Via the Internet Irene is communicating with other autistic people. With Irene's added confidence it is not long before she uses her new communication system to reiterate that she wants to live on her own. With her circle of family and friends in place and all supporting her plan, the process is under way and Irene will soon move into a flat in a supported living environment, not far from St John's. There she will have round-the-clock support, i.e. somebody living close who will be 'on call'. Irene will be able to call that person from anywhere via her communication board; when she rings from her home, that will automatically be registered by the receiver. They are looking into other 'intelligent' modifications to make in her new home to maximise her ability to cope on her own.

Irene and Kumar are both involved in piloting an innovative development of the Autism Alert idea, which is being tried out for use at home in its initial phase. Like many other people on the autism spectrum they both sometimes get into bad trouble because they have distressed feelings which become very intense at great speed, and which rob them of speech. Other people 'read' the behaviours that accompany these feelings as being meaningful and unacceptable. If damage limitation is not effective at these times, the repercussions can be grave. Now they each have a 'biofeedback' ring, these tremble when stress levels are going rapidly up, identified by measuring chemical changes on the surface of the skin.

The biofeedback mechanism means people wearing the rings have a chance to 'catch' the emotional change and identify it as mounting stress before it has peaked. At that point self-monitoring may be possible, but effective communication is unlikely. To deal with that issue another technical innovation has been developed in the shape of a reddish purple LED display, a couple of inches across, inconspicuous until struck – when it starts to flash. Probably most people in the world know that a flashing purple light usually means 'Stop!' Everyone who spends time at home with Irene or Kumar has had the meaning clearly explained: back off, and allow recovery time!

When the ring trembles its message about rising stress, the idea is that there is a choice to strike the flashing alert badge – a very easy action to take even when stressed. When people see the flashing light they understand this as a warning signal. The red light stops flashing after half a minute but continues to be lit, then it changes to orange/amber after five minutes, usually long enough for most people to recover some capacity. Both Kumar and Irene have used their LED displays. Kumar has had his awareness of his own mounting stress noticeably raised by the biofeedback and likes to wear the ring all the time. When his ring begins to tremble – as it does rather often – Kumar now rarely sets off his LED alert; he tries to calm himself down instead and enjoys getting the ring to stop its agitation as he stops his own. Irene has used her LED alert fairly often, and very much likes the effect it has on other people. They and everybody around them find that situations are far less likely to get out of control with these new technological aids than they used to. So far they are only using the LED alert around home – later on, if it is judged a success (which it promises to be) it will go into mass production and its launch will be accompanied with a major publicity campaign so that people in authority and members of the public are aware of its meaning.

Like Irene's, Kumar's life has moved on a long way. His talk to the staff at Irene's old home on using IT, and especially PowerPoint, was such a success that he has been employed to spread the word throughout all of Goodfolk's projects. In these meetings Kumar finds the fact that he is 'holding the floor' and has the right to speak and be listened to without interruption wonderfully satisfying. He no longer does these training sessions for £70 – though he is probably still a bargain, given how committed his performance is every time. His involvement in the Advisory Group and his work on the website have also taken him further towards being seriously employable. His success is a huge relief for his family; even his father moves from seeing Kumar as a shame on the family to seeing him as a blessing. His parents begin to discuss in earnest the possibility of finding

Kumar a suitable bride. To their surprise, instead of being grateful he tells them to forget it.

One of the people whose postings in the neurodiversity discussion Kumar often likes a lot, is a young woman called Sara. They start sending each other private emails as well as the public messages left on the discussion board. They share a lot of views, and they make each other laugh. They start speaking occasionally by phone. In July they will meet at this year's Autscape – one of the annual retreats-cum-conferences for autistic people which have been happening in the UK since 2005 and are held in the depths of the English countryside. Sara has seen Kumar's lifestory and knows that he has always liked the idea of going riding; after Autscape they will spend a day together, learning to ride.

Kumar dreams.
They all dream.
We all dream.

Chapter 9

Taking Control of Time

A Step-by-step Guide to Making an Interactive Calendar

Not knowing for sure what's happening next is a recurrent and sometimes severe problem for all three of our heroes. Kumar, Irene and Marie – like anyone else – all benefit from having a reference for what is happening and what is going to happen. Calendars of whatever form are purpose-built to this end. What advantage will we gain by putting a calendar into a PowerPoint show as suggested in this chapter? The main gain can be summed up as 'depth' – everything on the PowerPoint calendar can potentially be hyperlinked, and so be structured and inquired into more deeply than any paper calendar. Another significant gain is flexibility – options can be easily shown, choices recorded and changes made, as needed. It is also infinitely extendable – if questions arise they can be pursued and their answers incorporated as and when. Everything can be vividly and specifically illustrated too – even with moving images and sound with the help of a digital camera. 'Just in case' options can be built in to every day and fully examined and considered well in advance. That way the unexpected can be transformed from something shocking to something acceptable or at worst regrettable.

Kumar's problems with time seem even worse for him than they are for the others, because he has a long view as shown by the wall chart on his bedroom wall, and has worries about events far in the future. However, as we have seen, the main trouble for Kumar is the same as it is for Irene, i.e. an extremely high level of anxiety. Uncertainty makes us all anxious, but both of them may obsessively and repeatedly need reassurance about coming events. Irene knows about Easter, her birthday and Christmas – she used to have a picture of a Christmas tree which she would bring to staff, asking them to hurry it up. She always knows the day and time of her scheduled massage too, and if staff are not taking the appropriate steps Irene will stand anxiously by the door holding her coat. Marie just needs a bit of help these days keeping on track, prompts from her phone and a clear schedule on her calendar provide that help.

Like most of us, each of these people has a moderately predictable week with some regular scheduled activities. But because none of them has a job or a young family to look after, their days tend to be underoccupied compared with most people's. Yet another advantage of having a calendar on-screen as outlined below is that it becomes an intrinsically interesting object. An on-screen calendar can go from being a neutral format for structured time to being a personal exploratory and creative space which actively occupies time. We will start with the bare structure as though it is just a paper thing, then fill in that structure with help from Marie, Irene and Kumar.

To make a basic calendar

Step one: Preparing yourself

Open PowerPoint and it will automatically start a new show. If you've never used PowerPoint before then your first step should be to sit down, open the programme, and play – do things and see what happens, explore: nothing bad will happen!

Step two: Preparing a week-long calendar

Create a folder called 'Calendar Template' and save every file you make in this process into that folder. Start making sure that the slide layout chosen is blank – this means that you stay in control of what goes where, rather than having frequent annoying surprises as the clever software outsmarts you and expands, shrinks, or moves what you are making. In the dropdown menus along the top of the screen there is one headed 'Insert'. There is also an icon which will say 'Insert Table' when you move your cursor over it. The dropdown menu has the same option but invites a wider numerical range. We want to draw a table with seven columns, one for each day of the week. How many rows we have will depend on how many different times of day we want to discriminate between. Three basic divisions might be enough for most people, others might want to mark finer portions of time. For now, choose seven columns and three or four rows from the 'Insert Table' menu.

They will arrive looking like Figure 9.1. There are two ways of changing that. One is to select the table then identify a corner and click and drag it, which will stretch the whole table to fill up exactly the space you choose (this is the same procedure as resizing a picture). By clicking onto its active points you can change an object or table's size or proportions – the cursor arrow will turn into a two-way arrow at these active points; if it becomes a four-way arrow then you can move the whole object the cursor is reacting to by clicking and dragging it. Alternatively, select the table and right click on it, you will be given a menu with

Figure 9.1 Table

'Table Properties' at the bottom. Click on 'Table Properties' and choose the 'Row' tab at the top of the window, tick 'Specify height' and choose 'Exactly' from the drop down options (if you leave it set to 'At least' it will stretch and may be inconsistent – you may not mind that). Now you can choose exactly what size the sections of your table will be. Columns will automatically divide the horizontal space evenly unless you over-ride that. Now click on the page just above the table and insert another table, this time only one row deep. This will be where you enter the names of the days of the week.

OK, now we have a starting place. We can put in everything which happens repeatedly into this basic calendar format. So we fill in the names of all the days of the week across the top, and we will name the regular meals in the sections of a day – for now just in one column, which we will copy and paste into all the other columns after Step four (to save keystrokes).

Step three: Preparing to hyperlink

Now we're going to take advantage of one of PowerPoint's niftiest tricks, the possibility of linking from absolutely any object, word, text box, picture, callout (in 'Autoshape'), etc. to other documents or to other places in the same document. Do Ctrl+M and a new slide will appear, choose the slide template that features a title only and put the word 'Sunday' into its title slot, then press Ctrl+M another six times entering the successive days of the week into each slide's title slot. Next do Ctrl+N and a new show will open, enter the word 'Breakfast' into its title slot, save it as 'Breakfast' and repeat this process for 'Lunch' and 'Supper' too. That makes three shows waiting to be developed, and linked from and to the weekly calendar.

Note that this process of linking to meals, etc. could be contained in one presentation. But that might become over-complicated and difficult to manage.

Step four: Inserting hyperlinks

Every word in this calendar is to be a hyperlink, i.e. an area of the screen which will allow you to move at once to another digital location. Highlight the word 'Sunday' – now you can turn it into a hyperlink. Go through the 'Insert' dropdown menu which includes 'Hyperlink'; or you can just press Ctrl+K when you have highlighted a word or object. Either of those procedures will open a window inviting you to identify or anchor to the place to which you wish to link. This time, you will assign the slide called 'Sunday' created at Step three as the target to be linked to via the hyperlink. Now when the show runs, the cursor will turn into a little hand when it rolls over the word Sunday; click when that happens and it will immediately open the Sunday slide. Carry on with the days of the week, each of which links via the 'Place in This Document' or 'Anchor' option – in the Insert hyperlink window – to the day slides further on in the show. Breakfast, lunch and supper each get a whole show of their own, so you link to them via the 'Existing File or Web Page' option in the 'Insert hyperlink' window.

Step five: Completing the basic calendar outline

So far the meals are only named in one column. Highlight that column, then copy it by pressing Ctrl+C or opening the 'Edit' dropdown menu and choosing 'Copy'. Then paste it either by pressing Ctrl+V or by choosing 'Paste' from the 'Edit' menu, click into each successive column and paste in the contents you have copied into each. Now we have a week-long calendar which looks more or less like Figure 9.2.

Now we have the basic outline of Marie's week, Irene's week, Kumar's week – anyone's week – waiting to be filled in and developed.

Sunday	Monday	Tuesday	Wednesday	Thursday	Friday	Saturday
Breakfast	Breakfast	Breakfast	Breakfast	Breakfast	Breakfast	Breakfast
Lunch	Lunch	Lunch	Lunch	Lunch	Lunch	Lunch
Supper	Supper	Supper	Supper	Supper	Supper	Supper

Figure 9.2 Calendar

Step six: Making a year of weeks

Next there's a dreary but simple repetitive task: do 'Save As' (from the 'File' dropdown menu) 52 times naming each one 'Week 1', 'Week 2' right up to 'Week 52'. This is boring but easy: open the 'File' dropdown menu then pick 'Save As' for each one. You then will just have to change the final digit for each save – i.e. 'Week 1', 'Week 2' etc., and soon you will have a whole year of weeks, each of which is its own potential PowerPoint show.

Step seven: Creating a year calendar, making a basic month

Next we need to create another new PowerPoint show, this time it will be for a whole particular calendar year, month by month – let us say, 2006. Once again we use the 'Insert Table' option from the 'Insert' dropdown menu, but this time we request six rows as well as seven columns. (That may seem more than you could possibly need, but it is so that the days of every month can be smoothly fitted in without tucking in the end days of some months back at the month's beginning – as many wall calendars do.) Make sure it is the size and in the position that you want – highlight it and 'drag' one of the corners to expand it, keeping its proportions.

Next, we need to insert a table just one row deep and seven columns wide. We want that to sit above the top row of the larger table. When you enter it, it will probably appear plastered over the month table. Don't worry! Once again, just highlight it then click on its active points to push or pull its borders to get it the right size, then click and drag it to the right position, using the key strokes ('→' or 'Ctrl →') to make fine adjustments. Once you have it in your chosen position, aligned with the successive days in the columns below, then enter in names of the days of the week.

Step eight: Discriminating the weeks

We are now going to make a text box to embrace one week of the month calendar at a time. This will enable us later on to number the weeks and hyperlink them to the numbered week PowerPoint shows we have already made. You can do this either through the 'Insert' dropdown menu, clicking on 'Text Box', or by clicking on the text box icon on your screen. You want it to fit along one seven-column wide row, i.e. horizontally, and the letters 'wk' need to be inserted into it in a small font size (e.g. 12 point) and the text alignment set to the right. You want to stretch the text box so the abbreviation 'wk' will appear just to the right of the rightmost column, while the left border lines up with the left edge of the table. Now highlight that text box and copy and paste it a total of six times to match the six rows. When you first paste these in they will conform to the size and shape of the first text box you made, but they will plonk themselves down in a stepped, overlapping, sequence (a bit like a hand of cards). No worries, they will move at your command – just click and drag each one onto its own row. If you need fine adjustments, remember the 'Ctrl' and cursor keys (the arrows on your keyboard) will give you those.

Step nine: Making the months add up to a year

Next we are going to turn this PowerPoint display of a single potential month into a calendar for a whole year. Copy the slide you've made: Ctrl+A will highlight its contents, and Ctrl+C will copy them. Then create 11 new slides by doing Ctrl+M then Ctrl+V 11 times – Ctrl+M makes a new slide, Ctrl+V pastes in the contents you copied. Each of these slides will have more than enough days for any given month and these will need to be filled in according to the allocation of days in 2006. Each slide will be named after its month, and then the right numbers entered. Entering in all the numbered days is another rather tedious, repetitive, but undemanding task. Using the tab key will make it slightly easier as it will move you to the next square in each table. You may wish to single out bank holidays in some way, as many calendars do. It will be helpful to have a paper calendar in front of you to help you keep track of all this. Put in the names of each month in a text box above each slide.

You could save a lot of key strokes with a bit of cunning by copying and pasting the numbers of any months which start on the same day of the week. For example, in all non-leap years February, March and November all start on the same weekday, and so do January and October. But of course the months are not all the same length so they would each need to be adjusted to ensure the numbers stop on the right day. Plodding on by hand might be less effortful since it probably requires less thought. Your choice depends on your personal path of least resistance.

Step ten: Hyperlinking to the numbered weeks

This is the last really tedious task, and you don't really have to do it all at once. You could keep just ahead of yourself as the weeks go by, highlighting the next week's text box, inserting the week's number, then hyperlinking the whole text box to its matching weekly calendar. However, there are advantages to having the whole year prepared. People may easily take an interest in events like birthdays or festivals or the start and finish of college terms, etc., months ahead of the scheduled events and if you want to encourage exploration you should maximise the fun value of the calendar and make sure that the future can be discovered or outlined with ease. What is more, at the next step we will store this as a prototype and save ourselves much future work that way.

So ideally we create a hot link (hyperlink) for every week of the year, linking it to its matching PowerPoint show. We also need to insert the week's number next to the word 'wk' in that week's text box (for reference purposes). It is important to note that the way the calendar is arranged means that for most transitions from one month to another the week's number will need to be repeated. For example, January ends on the Tuesday of the fifth week of the year, February starts on the Wednesday of the fifth week of the year, so the first week of February and the last week of January will both be wk5.

Step eleven: Copying and individualising the calendars

Now open your Windows Explorer (or Finder in Mac), e.g. by clicking on 'My Documents' in the 'Start' menu or elsewhere. Choose 'Folders' view (in the toolbar at the top) and now in the 'File' dropdown menu choose 'New', and then 'Folder', now we create *four* differently named folders: Marie's year, Irene's year, Kumar's year and Prototype year, which will be left undeveloped as basic material for future years (yes the daily numbering will have to be changed per year, but everything else will be retained and re-usable). Then highlight the 52 weeks of PowerPoint shows and the year calendars and copy the lot four times, once into each of those new folders. We now have a basic format which can be developed individually to suit anyone. Hyperlinks will lead to other shows in the same folder. If you need to be super-careful to avoid confusion, you could add an initital to the file names in every individualised set, but so long as they retain their distinct folder location there should not be a problem with identical file names.

Steps twelve to infinity: Bringing the calendars to life

OK, so now we have a whole lot of bits of calendar which look much like their paper equivalents. At the moment the main significant difference between our calendars and bits of paper is that these 'pages' can find each other automatically because they have been electronically tagged. The other main difference between this digital format and a piece of paper is just the potential to be enlivened. Illuminated manuscripts have nothing on the richness and depth of detail we can use to light up these pages.

So, we have a table to fill in for each person. It won't make it look or feel any more complicated to get infinite depth into this two-dimensional object. We will start by looking at representing the massage Irene has on Thursdays. Instead of – or as well as – the word 'massage' we can find an image to convey the idea of it. There are lots of ways we could do that. We could use a digital camera and take pictures of the outside and inside of the place Irene has her massage, we could take pictures of the masseuse. But none of those would appear very clearly in the small space available on the week calendar. An alternative would be to find something which could make a small meaningful symbol. This is where Google Image Search can be just what you need. You will immediately appreciate the scope for finding things out without moving from your 'port'. There you are between your four walls, on your own, and you can explore and investigate just about anything in the known universe without moving more than your hands and your eyes. Anyone who can write can do this. There is also a facility for searching for images: below the word Google there is an option named 'Images'; click on that and decide what to look for. In this case, we need an impersonal image which will somehow sum up a massage: if you look for 'hands massage' you will find the set of images which combines hands with massage. When I did it, it came up with 3320 relevant pictures, some photos, some symbols, some symbols with 'added meaning' such as the 'Heavenly Hands' logo with starry magic flowing from its fingertips and some words; another with simple hands which could be handprints and suggest hands pressing down; others are obviously bare flesh, some a little suggestive – but most firewalls, etc. will ensure that seriously lewd images will not come up.

When it comes to choosing which of those images to use, much the best thing to do will be to sit down with Irene – if she will just come over and sit down to take a look, she can choose. However, knowing Irene, she will at best linger round the outside of the room with the computer in it unless something attracts her to it strongly enough. The whole project will be of much less value if it is not developed with Irene's personal involvement. So, we need to find a way to lure her into engaging with the strange set of objects which constitute a computer. For example we can insert an attractive sound effect such as the sound of breaking glass which can be found for free on the www.a1freesoundeffects.com website (search for 'wav free download' in Google for other sites). Such sounds can be pasted in one at a time into the slides for each day of the week, so that when the slide opens the sound will automatically play. Or the sounds can be inserted so that each one will play every time you click on it, or an image – for example of broken glass – can be hyperlinked to it.

Now we can get the Google Image Search up and see how Irene reacts to the various images, we can click on them one at a time and see them full size. We could save any which seemed to interest her, and revisit them at leisure. Irene seems to like the image in Figure 9.3.

Figure 9.3 Massage

So we'll choose that pair of hands to insert into Irene's weekly calendar to stand for Massage. Don't forget how important it is not to *replace* words with images. If someone does not already read then there is no harm at all in giving them examples of written words to learn from. We are supposed to be encouraging lifelong learning! And if someone can already read we have to remember we are not supposed to be de-skilling people! Let's encourage reading wherever possible. The point of adding pictures, moving pictures and sounds is not to supplant the written word, but to enliven it. To keep the words and still use the image at a small enough scale to fit into the calendar, highlight it and choose the 'Format Image' option. There should be a way of altering the transparency of the image, and making it about 70 per cent transparent will mean that the word easily shows through. You will also need to activate a corner of the highlighted image so as to shrink the image down to fit the column.

Now we'll link both the word and the image to a slide further on. Put a new slide at the end with the heading 'Massage'. The simplest way to link to that is by inserting the number of the massage slide into the window which opens when you highlight the word 'Massage' and the hands image in turn, and press Ctrl/Apple+K to add the hyperlink. While the hands make a conveniently small 'icon' for the weekly calendar, the massage slide itself could include much more. For example it could include the bare flesh image with hands working at it, to which Irene is also drawn. It could include a picture of the masseuse, captioned with her name – we can take a photo of her, of her 'therapy rooom', or of the front of her house. With a digital camera we can do all that and even film leaving home and arriving at the massage clinic. We could record the masseuse saying 'Welcome' so that it plays when Irene clicks on her picture. We can find a map of the massage clinic's neighbourhood, or of the route from home to there. This page could get mighty crowded… We can start another show any time.

There could be a whole new PowerPoint show about massages with this slide as its starting point. All we have to do is press Ctrl+A within the massage slide, to highlight everything, then Ctrl+C (Mac equivalent: Apple A, Apple C, etc.) to copy it all, then Ctrl+N to start a new PowerPoint presentation, and finally Ctrl+V to paste in what we copied. This is a very useful sequence of key strokes which you may find you use often.

We could also have separate shows for every meal: breakfast, lunch, supper which those words would link to. And each of those could be stuffed in turn with further links as and when interesting possibilities occur. Similarly, we can create a whole show for family members. For that we would want them to lend as many photos as they can find, old and new (or use the ones in the lifestories – see Chapter 3) – which we would then scan in as needed, label, and hyperlink to other family members, older or younger. We might make a bit of a family tree too.

Most weeks will include three trips to the day centre, so on one of those days we can map out the trip there and the trip back, with approximate timings – and then duplicate that result on the other two days. We could show a small image of the bus and link that to a slide further on (new slides can be added at any time; it is best to do that at the end so as not to confuse hyperlinks to numbered slides) with a view of the outside and the inside of the bus (or the alternative buses if there's more than one). We could do the same thing with pictures of home and of the day centre, place them at the beginning and end of a statement such as 'Bus arrives between 9 and 9.30 to go to the day centre' or 'Bus leaves at about 3.15 to take everyone home'. Again, the words and/or pictures can be linked to another slide, which in turn… It's up to you to decide – the options are only limited by your imagination!

In the day slide for each day of the week we can put the day's specifics which vary from week to week. Each week will be saved separately under its own name. So on each day of the week we can have a text box beside lunch and supper which would say:

What's for lunch?	What's for supper?

To insert a text box you can go to the 'Insert' menu and choose 'Text Box', then click anywhere on the page and drag the cursor a little way diagonally. The small box can receive as much text as you want but may need to be pulled to a larger size, by clicking and dragging on a corner, just as you do with pictures.

For each week, current decisions made or meals eaten can be recorded in these text boxes – we will sit down and do it with Irene as far as possible, don't forget these are *her* choices. Even if she never joins in, in the sense of pressing keys or handling the mouse, it is important to ensure that she is involved to the maximum in the decisions recorded, and is aware that they are being so recorded. Obviously enough all appointments and one-off events can be entered into the yearly, weekly and daily calendars (there is no automatic way to make sure they appear in all three, so this must be done manually). The daily calendars will make a framework for logging each day's events easily.

When it comes to birthdays and feast days, we can really 'go to town', for example with sound effects such as sleigh bells, footsteps on crunching snow, Christmas carols. We can even have animated cards programmed to arrive on those special days, as we shall see later. Irene may eventually be able to check for herself how far it is till Christmas. It will be a good idea to mark each day as it comes, perhaps by clicking and dragging a picture, for example of Irene herself or an icon of her choosing, to represent her movement through time. After a while Irene finds she gets a kick out of doing it herself. She is also so interested in checking out when the next festival is that she spends a while obsessively running through the months in the year calendar until she is finally convinced that the sequence of days is passing in an orderly fashion and, for example, that Christmas really is getting closer.

For now we'll leave Irene with her enlivened weekly calendar. The same basic techniques can be used to develop Marie's and Kumar's calendars in various ways. Both Kumar and Marie have a long overview with more detail than Irene. Kumar is enrolled in a college course and needs terms and holidays recorded on his calendar. He will be given a timeline for his coursework, and will find it helpful to have those deadlines incorporated into his calendar. He also, like Irene, finds the orderly progression of the days in the year calendar intrinsically pleasing and likes being able to look ahead and know that certain events are almost guaranteed to happen.

Marie does not appear to have that sort of time-based anxiety – she has been experiencing for many decades the grinding progression of hours into days, days into weeks, and weeks into years which makes our perception of time. However, Marie is very concerned not to miss any of the birthdays she has always been so well known for assiduously recognising and celebrating. Remember, Marie's short-term memory is poor, but her long-term memory remains excellent and she knows who all her cousins and their spouses are, and all their children now grown up. Even though the next generation, born in the last four or five years, have not made any very clear impression on her, she has their birthdays in her birthday book.

Chapter 10

How to Get IT Right

Tackling the Technical Aspects of Using Computer Equipment

Fortunately for our trio, and for everyone else who uses IT equipment, computers are much more reliable than they used to be and don't often 'crash' with the awful consequences that you lose all of the work which you have done in that session. In modern computers, if the computer does crash and you restart it, it will usually open into the document on which you were last working. Sometimes, however, the computer 'freezes', that is, nothing moves and you can't move the cursor with the mouse or navigate around the page in any way. If this happens, be patient and wait for a while as it is likely that the computer is 'busy' working on the last instruction you gave it. If the problem persists hold in the on/off button until the machine resets (starts again) or press Ctrl+Alt+Del at the same time.

One way of ensuring that you do not lose your work is to save it frequently. A good habit to get into is using the 'Save As' feature as soon as you start a document and once you have given the document a name and location, you just need to click on the quick save icon at regular intervals or press Ctrl+S. Marie learned this when she once lost a whole morning's work when a visitor pressed the 'power off' button without saving her work first.

There are a few more golden rules to follow so that you can limit the damage. One day Kumar decided to 'tidy up' his Desktop as this is where many of his documents had been saved so that he could find them easily. However, he was very upset when he accidentally deleted a file that he needed. Luckily, Kumar knows about the 'Recycle Bin' ('Trash' on Mac) which stores files which have been deleted until you actively 'empty' it. Therefore Kumar was able to go to the Recycle Bin and restore the file to his computer.

Another useful feature for the staff working with Marie which helped them to find the most recent document Marie had been working on is one built into all Microsoft applications. If you return to your work in Word (or any of the Microsoft Office applications) and you can't remember what you called the last document you were working on, you can find this by going to 'File' and right at the bottom of the menu will be a list of the last few files on which you have worked.

We have already seen that personal computers and peripheral equipment, such as printers, scanners and digital cameras are far more reliable than they were just a few years ago. However, what should you look for when buying IT equipment? There is no easy answer to this question as the technology is changing all the time and what is an excellent buy today may not be the best solution tomorrow. Perhaps the wisest way to buy equipment is to set a budget and then to think about what specifically that piece of equipment will be used for and then do your research either on the Internet, buying a computer magazine or looking around the shops and comparing prices.

There are many different makes and styles of printers on the market and available through many outlets on the high street, Internet sites or purchased from magazines. Before purchasing a printer you should consider what it will be used for. Initially this may seem a superfluous question, but if you are going to produce a newsletter for a wide circulation on a regular basis you will definitely choose a different printer from the one chosen by a person whose hobby is photography and who prints out their photographs in a high definition to display in a gallery or to sell. So what features would you look for? You may want to print your newsletter on A3 paper so that you just need to fold it and not staple it. This will limit your choice of printer and will probably increase the cost, but it will save you a great deal of time in the future. You may also want to consider whether the printer has a duplex option; this means that it will print on both sides of the paper. If you want to produce 'business' or personal cards you will need to check that your chosen printer can handle thin card as well as paper. It may be that you will be posting many items, in which case a printer which will also print a variety of sizes of envelope may be useful. There are many magazines which publish consumer tests and these will give a comparison of the costs of consumables and printing time. You may also need to consider the size of the printer and where it is to be used. An A3 printer will take up more space than an A4 printer. You can now get some very small printers, these are often not as robust but are ideal for someone who wants a 'portable' option. Currently, there are many printers available which combine printing, scanning and photocopying. These can be useful for the small home office, as they take up less space. Prices vary greatly depending on the number of features and the quality of the output.

That leads us onto scanners. Scanners are now very affordable and for our trio who want to continue to add to their lifestories a scanner is an essential. They are useful too for keeping digital copies of all essential documentation.

Many homes now keep copies of their utility bills in digital format, saving space and making filing easy! Scanners also vary in size and price and again it is a good idea to read the latest consumer tests in a computer magazine and to look at additional features, for example some scanners also have the facility to scan in negatives so that you can produce photographs from them.

Another piece of IT equipment that is an essential these days is a digital camera. When these first became popular getting photographs from the camera to the computer was a complex process requiring special connections and software. With the introduction of USB and Windows XP the process is much simpler and more manageable and with additional hardware (small cards) the digital photographer can happily snap away for some time before having to 'download' the photographs. As with all other IT equipment, the number of digital cameras available is mind-blowing! The range in any camera shop changes very quickly. Here again you should be very clear about the price ceiling you are willing to pay (and not be tempted to exceed this!) and the purpose of your purchase. Many people are tempted by the high specification of the photographs but for most of us four million pixels is sufficient, don't forget that the higher the resolution the more memory-intense the photos are, and this also makes them more difficult to email to friends and family. Many digital cameras now have a movie feature and allow the user to take short video clips. This can be very useful when compiling a lifestory which contains just brief glimpses of a person's activities. However, if you would prefer to have mainly movie you should consider buying a camcorder with a still photograph feature. Take time to check the quality of the zoom if you think that this feature will be important to you. If you like to take photos from a distance, for example, I know of one staff member who feels that she gets better photos when those being photographed are not aware of her close presence (though they have consented in principle), you may want a camera with a powerful zoom. Another thing to check is whether the camera has a rechargeable battery – which in the long run can be a cheaper option but means that you have to remember to take the battery charger with you when you go on holiday. Lastly, many people choose a camera because they like the look of it or the size. There are really tiny cameras around now which suit some people, but we are really looking at what would be suitable for using with people who may have limited fine motor control, and for them using a tiny camera with a very small viewing mechanism and small screen to see the photos once they have been taken may be very frustrating.

One digital camera which has been around for some years now and has proved very popular with people with learning disabilities is the Sony Mavica. This uses a floppy disk (or in some models a CD-Rom) as a storage device. This makes it extremely versatile as no additional wires or software is needed and the photos can be viewed, stored and used on any computer. It has a very simple telephoto feature and can take photos in a variety of formats such as black and white, sepia as well as the normal colour option. Also the chunky, robust camera is easy to use and has a large viewing screen. It is well worth considering this option when buying a digital camera.

We have already considered digital camcorders. There is a huge range coming in all shapes, sizes and prices. You will need to consider carefully which camera to buy and take advice from others who are already using cameras. It's like everything else: you don't know what features are most useful until you've used them. As important as the camera you choose is the software you use to edit the video clips. There is also a wide range of software at a variety of prices. There is one particular camera which is worthy of note here. That is the Digital Blue Movie Creator (www.playdigitalblue.com). This retails for under £100 and comes with simple editing software and has a variety of special effects. You can add titles and credits and transitions between scenes. You can also take still photos and send photos and movies as emails. The website has a demo and many ideas for getting started and a 'Hints and Tips' page. This is a very inexpensive option which has real potential for creating video for many occasions, such as showing how people integrate into drama or music sessions, and participate in group activities or give feedback on outings.

Having looked at the equipment which is available in mainstream outlets we should now consider the more specialist devices which support those people who cannot access computers through conventional mice and keyboards. A list of suppliers is included in this book (see Appendix 3). However, as suppliers realise that there are many input devices (equipment which allows data to be inputted to the computer) which are suitable for a whole range of people, these are beginning to become more widely available. At one time, for example, you would have needed to purchase a mouse for people with a disability from a specialist supplier, but now a whole range of different mice can be purchased to meet the needs of children, the elderly and to prevent repetitive strain injury (RSI). Mice now come in all shapes and sizes and it is a good idea to try them out before you buy them. There are organisations which help you such as AbilityNet (www.abilitynet.org.uk) which offer opportunities to visit them and try out a variety of alternatives. For some people an alternative to a mouse is a trackerball, a pointing device that is controlled by the movement of a large central ball and may reduce strain on the hands, arms or shoulders as the movement of the ball is controlled with the palm of the hand rather than the fingers. Both joysticks and trackerballs reduce the arm and hand movement required compared to using a traditional mouse on a mouse mat. This has many benefits, not least being that a user with limited mobility can have the device positioned exactly where they need it – for example cradled against the body or strapped to the arm of a wheelchair. Users suffering from RSI may also find a tracker ball or joystick less strain since the hand is supported in a more or less stationary position and there is reduced arm movement involved.

As computers have become popular so have the design of keyboards. There are in the region of two thousand different keyboards now being marketed. These include an extensive range of alternative keyboards, some of which are mainstreamed because of their claim to reduce RSI. When assessing the needs of a user you must consider how they will access information from the computer and input data. The type of keyboard may well be important in this assessment. For example, those people who have a visual impairment may be able to use a keyboard if the keys are larger and clearer than on a standard keyboard; for people who have difficulty reading text or have low literacy skills a lowercase keyboard may be useful; for others with difficulty with their fine motor control they may need a key-guard to help them to hit just one key at a time. You can also buy keyboard covers which protect keyboards against spills, dribble, dust, etc. These also come in high contrast colours to assist those with low vision. For some people hand movement may be difficult and there are a number of very small keyboards and also some designed to be accessed by one hand only.

One very different keyboard alternative which has many applications for people with learning disabilities is IntelliKeys (from www.intellitools.com). This alternative keyboard offers a range of access settings to meet the needs of a range of people with various disabilities as access settings can be customised for individuals. It works in conjunction with interchangeable overlays. An overlay is a printed sheet of paper or plastic that is placed over the touch-sensitive front panel of the IntelliKeys. Each overlay has a keyboard layout printed on it that may correspond to an on-screen document. Simply insert the appropriate overlay and begin working. Pressing a printed key on the overlay sends the desired information to your computer. Using overlays, a student can type letters, enter numbers, navigate on-screen displays, or execute menu commands.

For some people using a mouse or a keyboard of any description is either difficult or impossible. For them the answer to computer accessibility may be a switch. A switch is an input device which at any time can be either on or off. Where a user's physical movement is impaired, switches may be required to operate the computer. Many switches have been designed to meet the particular needs of disabled people. They come in many different shapes and sizes, and are designed to be operated by the hand, head, foot, etc. and work on a cause and effect mechanism. Unfortunately they do not work with all software as they require the software to scan (highlight one area of the screen at a time). Most new special needs software has switch access incorporated within it. The user can set the scan time to suit their needs.

A more expensive option to these input devices is a touch screen monitor. This is ideal for many people with cognitive disabilities who do not understand that entering data through a keyboard (or any other input device) causes a reaction on the screen. Most people are familiar with a touch screen monitor from using an ATM (Automated Teller Machine) in a bank. Improved technology allows people with learning disabilities to interact with the computer programme when using both mainstream and special needs software as it works wherever a mouse would. This gives people with severe learning disabilities the ability to be in control of programmes and is especially useful when they want to show their lifestory to others – any photograph (or even the whole page) can be made into a button so that once touched the programme progresses to the next slide.

Bibliography

123greetings.com (2005) 'Advertiser Benefits.' Online at www.123greetings.com/info/benefit.html

Aspinall, A. and Hegarty, J.R. (2001) 'ICT for adults with learning disabilities: an organisation-wide audit.' *British Journal of Educational Technology 32*, 3, 365–372.

Coleman-Martin, M.B., Heller, K.W., Cihak, D F. and Irvine, K.L. (2005) 'Using computer-assisted instruction and the Nonverbal Reading Approach to teach word identification.' *Focus on Autism and Other Developmental Disabilities 20*, 2, 80–90.

Cooper, J. (ed.) (2000) *Law, Rights and Disability*. London: Jessica Kingsley Publishers. (Comprehensive overview focused on rights in the widest sense.)

Department of Health (2001) 'Valuing People: A New Strategy for Learning Disability for the 21st Century.' London: The Stationery Office. Online at www.valuingpeople.gov.uk

Emerson, E., Magill, P. and Mansell, J. (eds) (1993) *Severe Learning Disabilities and Challenging Behaviours*. London: Chapman and Hall.

Grayson, A. (2004) Paper presented at 'Current Issues for Research and Practice' conference held at the Universiy of Durham, April. Paper was not written up for the conference proceedings.

Hogg, J. and Lambe, L. (1998) *Older People with Learning Disabilities: A Review of the Literature on Residential Services and Family Caregiving*. London: Mental Health Foundation. (Excellent round-up of literature.) Also available at www.learningdisabilities.org.uk/html/content/goldreview.pdf

Hudson, B., Dearey, M. and Glendinning, C. (2005) 'A New Vision for Adult Social Care: Scoping Service Users' Views.' *Research Works 2005-02*. Also available at *www.york.ac.uk/inst/spru/pubs/pdf/newvision.pdf*

jacquielawson.com (2005) 'Site Funding.' Online at www.jackielawson.com

Mirfin-Veitch, B. (2003) *Relationships and Adults with an Intellectual Disability: Review of the Literature Prepared for the [NZ] National Advisory Committee on Health and Disability to Inform its Project on Services for Adults with an Intellectual Disability*. Dunedin, NZ: Donald Beasley Institute. Available online at www.donaldbeasley.org.nz

Murray, D. and Lesser, M. (2004) 'Maximising Capacity and Valuing People.' *Current Issues for Research and Practice*. Autism Research Unit, School of Health and Natural Sciences: University of Sunderland.

Murray, D., Lesser, M. and Lawson, W. (2005) 'Attention, monotropism and the diagnostic criteria for autism.' *Autism 9*, 2, 139–156.

National Autistic Society (2005) 'Autism Alert Card.' Online at www.nas.org.uk/nas/jsp/polopoly.jsp?d=522

Parker, I. (2001) 'The Digital Age: Absolute PowerPoint.' The New Yorker, 28 May.

reactivecolours.org (2005) 'Program.' Online at www.reactivecolours.org

snow.utoronta.ca (2005) 'TTS.' Online at http://snow.utoronto.ca/prof_dev/ict/adaptive/week3/literacy2.htm

spired.com (2005) 'Important.' Online at www.spired.com/guide/law/online.htm

Shore, S. (ed.) (2005) *Ask and Tell: Self-Advocacy and Disclosure for People on the Autism Spectrum.* Kansas: Autism Asperger Publishing Company.

Thurman, S., Jones, J., and Tarleton, B. (2005) 'Without words: meaningful information for people with high individual communication needs.' *British Journal of Learning Disabilities* *33*, 2, 83–89.

Zarkowska, E. and Clements, J. (1991) *Problem Behaviour In People With Learning Disabilities: A Practical Guide to a Constructional Approach.* London: Chapman and Hall.

Appendix 1

Hints and Tips

When using PowerPoint

1 Making objects (pictures, symbols or text) into buttons in PowerPoint makes the presentation more interesting and allows the user to jump from one slide to any other slide in the show – rather than having to follow a linear progression.

2 When working on a lifestory (or any other presentation) it is good practice to create a folder to store all resources used so that you can find them easily should you need to replace them or use them again later.

3 When using buttons to go to different parts of a presentation don't forget to include a button on every slide to take you back to the front slide (or slide you have come from).

4 Once you have created one button you can copy it in the usual way and paste it to all other pages as appropriate. It will then be added to the page in exactly the same place and look the same. It will also carry with it the same 'actions', for example moving onto the next page.

5 When working on a multimedia lifestory, take a backup of it and the resources folder and keep separately from the computer. A good method of backing up work-in-progress is on a memory stick. Once completed give a copy of it to the individual on a CD.

6 You can narrate the whole (or part) of a PowerPoint show by using the 'Record Narration' feature in the 'Slide Show' menu.

7 To give emphasis to objects (such as text, quotations, photos, etc.) you highlight the object, and click on 'Add Effect' from the 'Custom Animation' feature from the 'Slide Show' menu. There is a range of animations providing more or less 'impact'.

8 To ensure that your presentation is professional and runs to time you can practice the timing using the 'Rehearse Timings' feature from the 'Slide Show' menu.

9   To access a PowerPoint presentation professionally in a meeting, save it as 'PowerPoint Show' in 'Save As' and save it to the Desktop. When you click on the shortcut on the Desktop it will open to the first slide full screen.

10 You can capture the image (often called a screen grab or print screen) on-screen at any time by holding down the 'Prt Sc' (or 'Print Screen') button on the computer keyboard (note sometimes you need to hold down the 'Ctrl' or 'Control' button at the same time). You then paste the captured image into a Microsoft application such as Word or PowerPoint.

11 To insert an object such as a circle to emphasise a point on a slide select 'Autoshapes' from the 'Drawing' toolbar (found under 'View'→'Toolbars'). A circle is found in the 'Basic Shapes' option. Click on it and then drag the shape out to the desired size/shape. You may need to highlight it, right click and 'Format Shape' to give it the desired attributes.

12 If you want to change the format of the font on every slide go to 'View'→'Master'→'Slide Master' and change the font there. Once you have closed the master slide the changes will affect every slide in the presentation.

When using any Microsoft application

13 If the computer 'freezes' (i.e. nothing moves – you can't move the cursor with the mouse) wait for a while (it may be that the computer is 'busy') – if the problem persists hold in the on/off button until the machine resets (starts again) – or hold down a combination of keys – Ctrl+Alt+Del for the same result.

14 Always save your document using the 'Save As' feature in the 'File' menu before starting work on a document. In this way you will be prompted to save your work when you leave the programme and it will save to the location you have identified.

15 Save your work frequently! If the computer crashes for any reason, such as a power-cut, you will only lose the work you have completed since the last time you saved it. You can do this by pressing Ctrl/Apple+S.

16 If you accidentally 'delete' a file you should be able to find that file in the 'Recycle Bin' and restore it to the computer.

17 If the computer 'crashes' and you restart it, it will usually open into the document on which you were last working.

18 Creating file names: when using a date in the filename if you put the date in the following order yyyymmdd at the beginning of the name, the documents (files or photos) will be stored in date order, e.g. '20040622 Irene party' will come before '20051105 Bonfire night' and so on.

Using the Internet

19 **Book-marking your favourite websites**
    When you discover a useful website you can 'book-mark' it by clicking on 'Favorites' on the menu bar. Now choose 'Add to Favorites' and you will be prompted to save the website into a folder. You can create new folders for every new area of interest. Next time you wish to access that website you just click on the link in Favorites and you will be taken directly to the page you saved.

Buying equipment

20 Always compare prices from a variety of sources – high street shops, Internet sites, computer magazines – and read consumer tests for comparisons of cost and features.

Appendix 2

Relevant Websites

Websites mentioned in the text

Note: All websites were accessed on 25 October 2005.

Government initiatives, legislation and documents

www.lsc.gov.uk – Learning and Skills Council; government-sponsored site with information about apprenticeships

www.publications.doh.gov.uk/learningdisabilities/access/ – download the accessible version of 'Nothing about us without us'

www.valuingpeople.gov.uk – the Valuing People white paper on learning disability

Autism

www.autismandcomputing.org.uk – research and campaigns about autism

www.autistics.org – information on autism from an autistic standpoint

www.autistics.org/library/ – autistic debate about treatment

www.gettingthetruthout.org – a powerful account of autism by a non-speaking autistic person, with pictures: persevere with it!

www.nas.org.uk/nas/jsp/polopoly.jsp?d=522 – link for getting the Autism Alert card from the National Autistic Society, UK

www.reactivecolours.org – a website with relaxing, undemanding, activities for people with autism

Disability

www.abilitynet.org.uk – an organisation which gives information to people with disabilities about computer aids

www.ldonline.org/ld_indepth/self_esteem/helplessness.html – a discussion on 'learned helplessness'

www.neurodiversity.com – a thought-provoking site with lost of links to research and to self-advocacy and personal accounts of people who are not neurotypical

www.symbolworld.org – a website developed for adult symbol users with areas for stories, learning and articles people submit. It has an online magazine called eLive which can be downloaded for a paper-based version to be read offline

Downloads: graphics, sounds and software

www.123greetings.com – free e-greetings cards

www.a1freesoundeffects.com/noflash.htm – free sound effects to download

www.clipart.co.uk – for clipart, graphics, buttons and animations

www.download.com – lots of useful free software to download

www.findsounds.com – for free downloads of sounds to make presentations and lifestories more interesting

www.flickr.com – a website for sharing photos with others with similar interests

www.freedownloadscenter.com – a website which offers free software downloads including prompting and messaging

www.graffitifonts.com/fonts.shtml – downloads of graffiti fonts to use with any word processor

www.jacquielawson.com – high quality animated ecards for a low flat-rate annual membership

www.laits.utexas.edu – free software downloads in many languages

www.multimap.com – to get maps of any area of the UK by inserting post codes or town and street names

www.partnershipforlearning.org/article.asp?ArticleID=888 – information about text-to-speech for children

www.promo.net/pg/ – lots of famous and important texts freely available to everyone in the world

www.readplease.com – download free text-to-speech software

www.shutterfly.com – a photo website similar to www.flickr.com

www.snow.utoronto.ca/prof_dev/ict/adaptive/ – information on downloading free text-to-speech programmes

www.tucows.com – free download website

www.uselessgraphics.com – for free downloads of graphics and animations

www.widgit.com – Widgit Software Ltd are producers of software which uses symbols to support text

Other

www.answers.com – wide-ranging information and definitions

www.friendsreunited.com – a website where you can look up old school friends and work colleagues

www.genesreunited.com – a website which helps people who are trying to complete their family tree or who are interested in genealogy

www.google.com – the world's favourite search engine

www.intellitools.com – flagship product is a programmable alternative keyboard

www.rebeccablood.net/essays/weblog_history.html – a history of blogs and blogging

www.spired.com/guide/law/online.htm – very useful advice about avoiding trouble using the Internet

www.playdigitalblue.com – simple and robust digital cameras and video recorders

www.thenthdegree.com – T-shirt website

Additional websites

Age Concern

www.ageconcern.org.uk/AgeConcern – offers 'Silver surfer' Internet training sessions

One for us

www.oneforus.com – a website for people who have a learning difficulty. It has information and stories about people with learning disabilities and shows people how to take more control over their own life

Becta (British Educational Communications and Technology Agency)

www.becta.org.uk – government agency promoting the use of information and communications technology. The site includes news, projects and resources on lifelong and special needs. Becta is the Government's key partner in the strategic development and delivery of its information and communications technology (ICT) and e-learning strategy for the schools and the learning and skills sectors

Check the Map

www.CheckTheMap.org – find all your learning disabilities services in the UK and Ireland. A resource section with loads of free, easy-to-play, online games

Ferl

www.ferl.becta.org.uk – Ferl is a service for practitioners in further education, sixth-form colleges and the post-16 sector. Ferl supports colleges in integrating Information and Communications Technology

More free clip-art

www.free-clipart.net

More free sounds

www.ilovewavs.com
www.simplythebest.net/sounds/WAV

Useful background reading

www.mencap.org.uk/download/mar02.pdf – to download information about 'The Bournewood Gap'

www.disability.gov.uk/dda/ – to download the Disability Discrimination Act

www.opsi.gov.uk/ACTS/acts1998/19980042.htm

www.publications.parliament.uk/pa/cm200304/cmbills/120/04120.i-vi.html – the Mental Capacity Bill

www.un.org/esa/socdev/enable/rights/ahc3reportadv.htm – the Draft UN Convention on the Protection and Promotion of the Rights and Dignity of Persons with Disabilities (2004)

Appendix 3

Resources

Augmentative and alternative communication (AAC)

Augmentative Communication in Practice: Scotland – An Introduction (1998)

This book, produced by Augmentative Communication in Practice: Scotland, provides a useful overview to the world of AAC. The sections cover AAC, both low-tech and high-tech, both children and adults, assessment and encouraging literacy development.

ISBN 1 89804 215 2 (2nd edition) published by The CALL Centre, Paterson's Land, Holyrood Road, Edinburgh EH8 8AQ Tel: 0131 651 6236 Email: call.centre@ed.ac.uk Website: www.callcentrescotland.org.uk

Communication without Speech: Augmentative and Alternative Communication Around the World, by Anne Warwick (1998)

This book is a highly accessible but very comprehensive introduction to AAC, with lots of practical tips and illustrations.

Published by ISAAC. Available from Communication Matters. Website: www. communicationmatters.org.uk

In Other Words

This video is an excellent introduction to the field of AAC, especially for parents, students, and professionals new to AAC.

Published by ISAAC. Available from The ACE Centre, 92 Windmill Road, Oxford OX3 7DR Tel: 01865 759800 Website: www.ace-centre.org.uk

Visual impairment

Royal National Institute of the Blind

105 Judd Street, London, WC1H 9NE

'See It Right': an RNIB project that gives practical advice to plan, design and produce accessible information especially for those with sight problems.

Tel: 020 7388 1266 Website: www.rnib.org.uk

Information and advice

AbilityNet

Address: Various around UK

Offer advice and information on assistive technology for anyone with a disability at home, in education or in employment. They run training courses and publish Helpsheets on their website which includes lists of resources and suppliers. Local AbilityNet offices will also lend resources so that you can try them out.

Tel: 0800 269545 Website: www.abilitynet.org.uk

CHANGE

Unity Business Centre, Units 19 and 20, 26 Roundhay Road, Leeds LS7 1AB

CHANGE have a picture bank of more than 500 pictures on CD-Rom. Many are used in printed materials.

Tel: 0113 2430202

Disability Rights Commission (DRC)

Helpline, FREEPOST, MID 02164, Stratford upon Avon, CV37 9BR

Easy read guidelines such as 'Making websites that are easy for everyone to use'.

Tel: 08457 622633 Website: www.drc-gb.org

Home Farm Trust (HFT)

Merchants House, Wapping Road, Bristol, BS1 4RW

'Let's be clear': a training video produced by HFT which aims to help staff to communicate with people with learning disabilities. With Griff Rhys Jones, it features real-life situations.

Tel: 0117 9302600 Website: www.hft.org.uk

Information Technology Can Help (ITCH) network

PO Box 28951, London, SW14 8WL

A network of volunteers who provide free computer support to disabled people. It is a programme of The British Computer Society (BCS).

Tel: 07985 779071 Email: info@itcanhelp.org.uk

Norah Fry Research Centre

Plain Facts Team, 3 Priory Road, Bristol, BS8 1TX

A magazine and tape for people with learning disabilities – findings about research projects.

Tel: 0117 9238137 Website: www.bris.ac.uk/Depts/NorahFry/PlainFacts/

The Symbol Trust

Woodlands Farm, Paddlesworth Road, Snodland, Kent, ME6 5DL

'Now we're talking': this video is about communication with people with Down's Syndrome from birth to age 30.

Tel: 01634 244000

Training

Clear Communication Training and Advice

853 Melton Road, Leicester, LE4 8EE

Clear offers training and consultancy to services to help them include people with learning disabilities through clear communication. Their team includes consultants with learning disabilities and speech and language therapists. They offer training and consultancy in areas such as making information easy to understand, consulting with people, communicating well in person-centred planning, organising accessible events, using signs and symbols and much more.

Tel: 0116 2128409

The HFT Karten CTEC (Computer Training, Education and Communication) *Centre*

HFT, Milton Heights, Abingdon, Oxon, OX14 4DR

HFT's ICT training centre offering training to staff and carers working with adults with learning disabilities. Their multimedia lifestory workshop is extremely popular.

Tel: 01235 835507 Website: www.hftcteccentre.org.uk

Hardware and software suppliers

Dolphin Computer Access

Dolphin Computer Access Ltd, Technology House, Blackpole Estate West, Worcester, WR3 8TJ

Best known for their access programmes for people with visual impairment, Dolphin now produce audio publishing software.

Tel: 01905 754577 Website: www.dolphinuk.co.uk

Granada Learning and Semerc

Granada Television, Quay Street, Manchester, M60 9EA

Suppliers of special needs software and hardware for all ages.

Tel: 0161 8272927 Websites: www.granada-learning.com and www.semerc.com

Inclusive Technology Ltd

Gatehead Business Park, Delph New Road, Delph, Oldham, OL3 5BX

Can buy Digital Blue Movie Creator from here. They supply many of the hardware and software solutions referred to throughout this book. See their website for training units

for use with people with disabilities. They provide a glossary of terms in ICT and a list of suppliers of equipment and training and free programmes to download.
Tel: 01457 819790 Website: www.inclusive.co.uk

Makaton

Makaton Vocabulary Development Project, 31 Firwood Drive, Camberley, Surrey, GU15 3QD
A unique language programme with a structured approach to communication with children and adults with learning disabilities.
Tel: 01276 61390 Website: www.makaton.org

Widgit Software Ltd

124 Cambridge Science Park, Milton Road, Cambridge, CB4 0ZS
Widgit offer software solutions for special needs. They have many resources freely downloadable from their website and links to websites for symbols users.
Tel: 01223 425 558 Website: www.widgit.com

Appendix 4

Helpsheets

Helpsheet A: PowerPoint for Windows XP[1]

Open PowerPoint and the following screen appears:

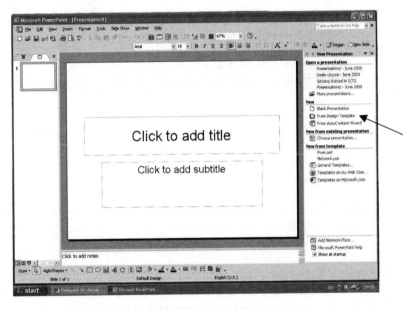

Click on 'From Design Template' under the 'New' menu.

---

1   The version of PowerPoint shown in these helpsheets is Microsoft PowerPoint 2003.

The following screen appears:

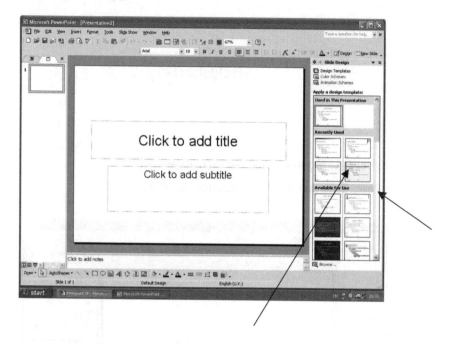

Double click on the design you would like to use.

Scroll down using the bar on the right to see more designs.

I've chosen the following 'design template' but you can choose any one you like. If you decide you would prefer another design just double click on your revised selection and it will replace your original selection.

Note: when you choose the design template it will not only put in the background design but will automatically format the text (i.e. use the same font style, colour and size) – however, you can change any of these when you want to.

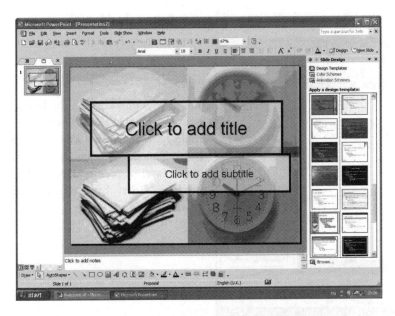

The first slide that is presented is the 'Title slide'. You now add the title of your presentation in the box that says 'Click to add title'. I have added 'My Lifestory'. Now add your name in the next box which says 'Click to add subtitle'.

Your slide will now look like this:

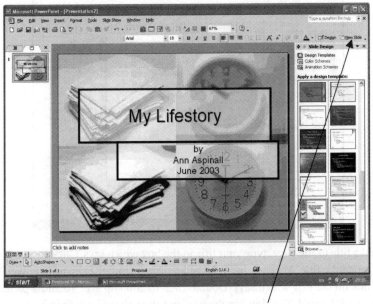

To add another slide – click on the 'New Slide' icon.

The following menu for layouts will appear on the right side of the screen:

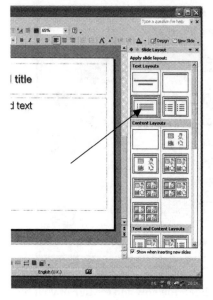

You now double click on the layout you want for the next slide, for example, you could have one with a title and a list of bullet points or one with a list of bullet points and a picture (see under the heading 'Other Layouts' by scrolling down).

For the example below I have chosen a layout with a picture and a list of bullet points, and the screen now appears like this:

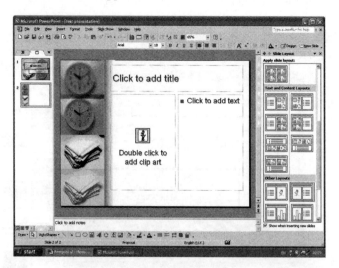

To add a title to the page, type your title in the box which says 'Click to add title' (I have typed the title 'My early life'). To add a picture from the clipart in PowerPoint just click on the box which says 'Double click to add clip art'. To add a picture of 'childhood' I typed 'Children' in the box and then clicked on 'Search'.

The following selection was available:

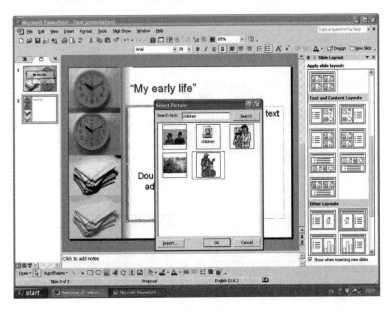

To import the picture of your choice select it (click on it) and then click 'OK'. The picture will appear on your page and you can change the size and position in the same way as you would in any other application (click on it and move it or drag out the edges or the corners to adjust the size).

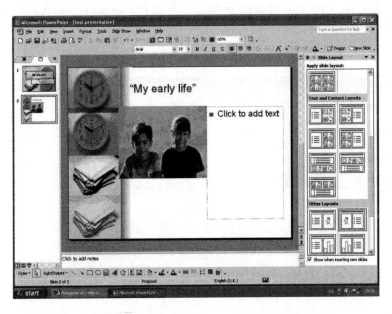

Now click in the box which says 'Click to add text' and type an appropriate sentence (I have chosen to add 'My brother is 2 years younger than me', etc.).

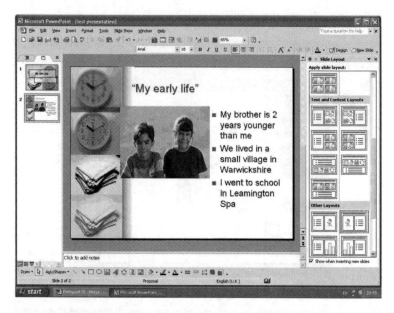

Now continue adding slides in the same way.

You can also add sounds to your slides

To do this select 'Insert' and then 'Movies and Sounds' from the dropdown menu. You can now choose: 'Sound from Clip Organizer' (gives you a choice of sounds which come with PowerPoint), or 'Sound from File' (you can insert any sound which is saved in a file on your computer or on a floppy disk), or 'Record Sound'.

Choose 'Record Sound' and the following menu appears:

blue
rectangle

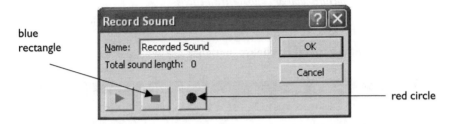

red circle

Click on the red circle and speak into the microphone.

When you have finished speaking click on the blue rectangle.

To hear the audio file click on the arrow (▶).

Click 'OK' and a small 'speaker' icon will appear in your presentation.

To view your presentation at any time
Click on the first slide down on the left-hand side of the screen so that it is highlighted (it has a blue outline):

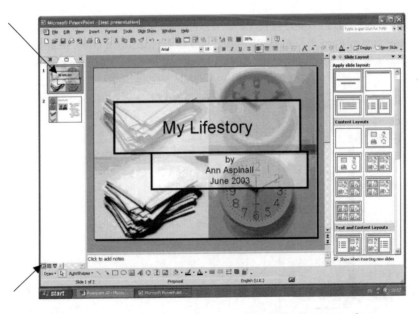

Then click on the icon which looks like a screen and the first page of your presentation will be shown (i.e. the title page). To move forward through the presentation click on the left mouse button. To listen to your recorded speech on the second slide click on the speaker button.

Adding some other features to your presentation

To make the text or pictures 'appear' with different effects

Click on the text and a new menu appears on the right of the screen.

Click on 'Add Effect' and then choose 'Entrance'.

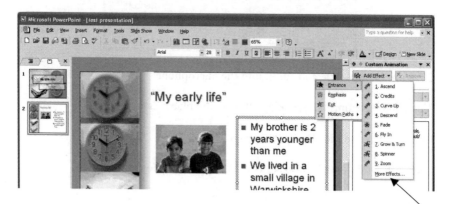

You now have a selection of effects to choose from. Try some of these – to see the effect click on the 'Play' button at the bottom of the screen if it doesn't show you automatically.

If you now want to add more effects – such as changing the colour of the text once you have moved onto the next bullet point – click on the down arrow next to the new dialogue box which has been opened on the right-hand side of the screen.

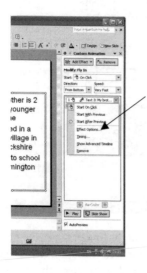

Click on 'Effect Options…'.

Now click on the down arrow (▼) next to 'After animation: Don't Dim'.

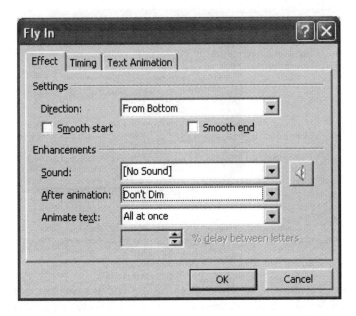

You can now choose a colour – the text will turn to this colour when you next click to reveal a new line.

How to insert buttons into PowerPoint

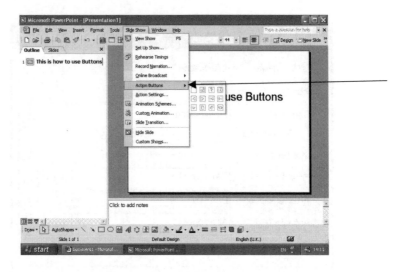

From the 'Slide Show' menu select 'Action Buttons' and then from the menu choose a button style and click on it. (There are buttons which already have actions attached to them, for example Home Page, Back and Forward.)

In this example, we will select the blank ('Custom') button.

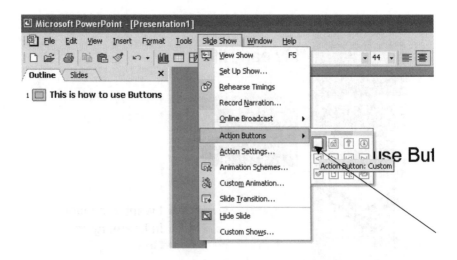

Next click onto the page where you want the button to be and you will get a cursor which looks like a plus (+). Now drag out the button until it is the size you want.

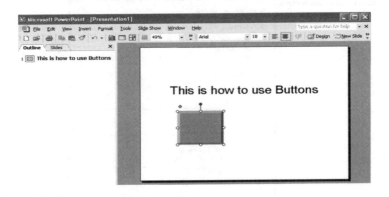

You will need to add an action to the button. To do this, either right click (i.e. click using the right-hand mouse button) and select 'Action Settings...' from the drop-down menu, or click on the 'Slide Show' menu at the top of the screen and, again, select 'Action Settings...'.

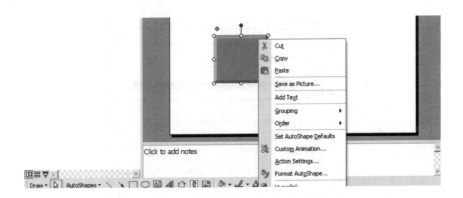

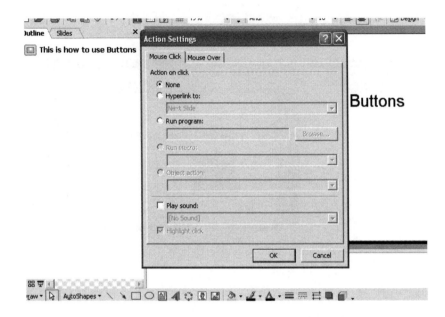

From here you can link to another page through the 'Hyperlink to' option. Your button then allows you to go directly to that other page, by clicking on it.

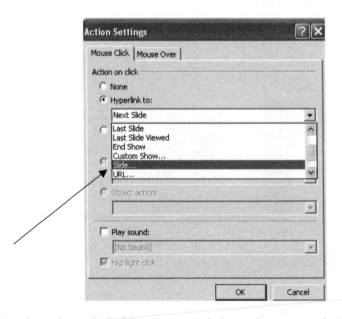

You choose here which slide you want to link your button to – obviously you need to have that slide already created.

You can change the colour, etc. of the button by right clicking on it and choosing 'Format AutoShape'.

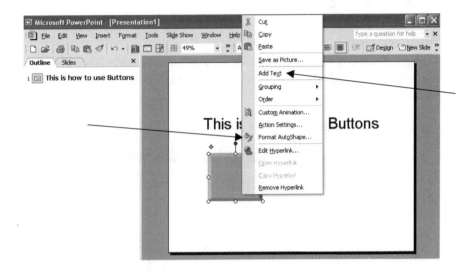

You can add text to the button by selecting the 'Add Text' option.

Helpsheet B: Slide Design in PowerPoint

You can change the background colours and features by changing either the template or the background.

Design templates

A design template is a pre-designed look for your presentation which comes with PowerPoint. It changes the background and style and colours of all text within the presentation.

Right click on the background of the slide.

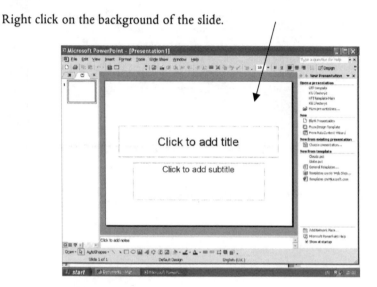

Left click on 'Slide Design...'

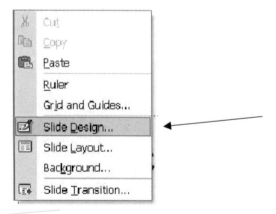

Choose a design template. Left click to apply it to your presentation.

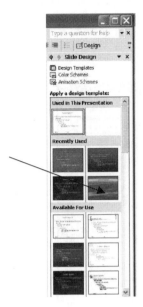

Tip: If you want just one slide coloured left click on the grey arrow to the right of the template. You will then have the option to apply to selected slides or all of the slides in your presentation.

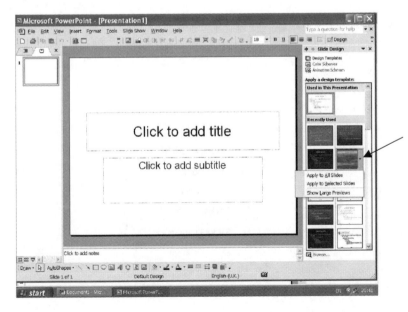

Coloured backgrounds (pages, action buttons, text boxes, etc.)

If you don't want one of the preset templates you can create your own colour scheme and backgrounds.

Right click on the object you want to change.

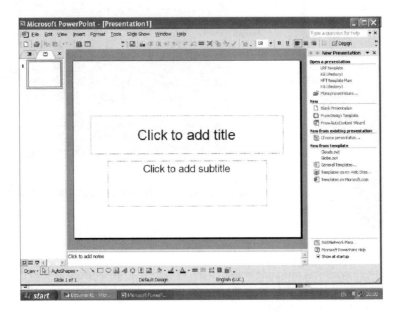

Left click on the 'Background...' button.

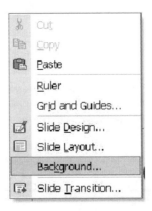

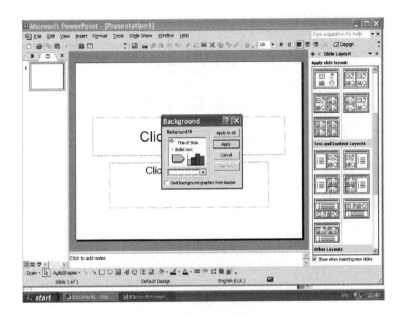

Left click on the down arrow to see the drop-down menu.

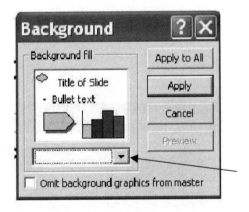

Left click on 'More Colors…'.

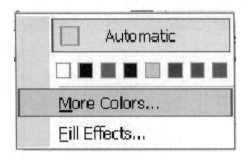

Left click on the colour you would like.

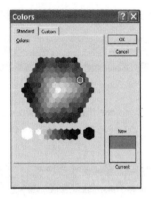

Left click on 'OK'.

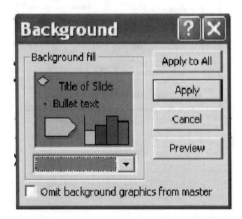

Left click on 'Apply', or 'Apply to All' if you want the same background on all your slides.

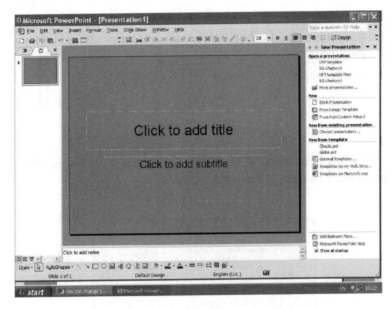

Fill Effects

Follow the same steps as for Coloured Backgrounds on pages 160–161, but instead of chosing 'More Colors…' click on 'Fill Effects…'.

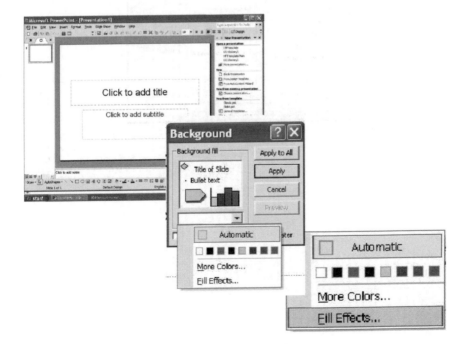

Within 'Fill Effects…' you can choose one of the following sections by clicking on the top tab.

You can change the background, for example, by gradient colours which allows you to choose two colours that blend into each other.

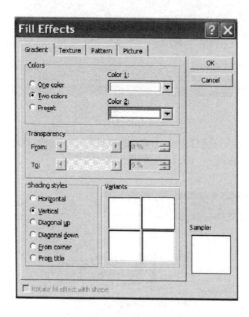

You can also change to a preset texture effect, pattern or picture by clicking on the relevant tab.

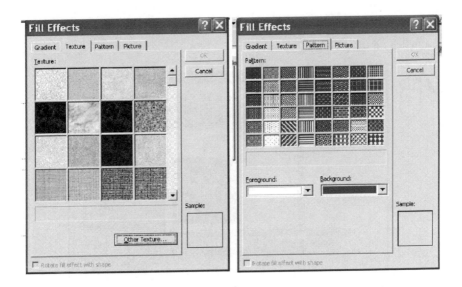

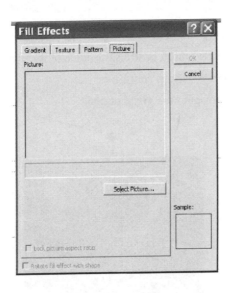

Helpsheet C: Editing and Cropping Photos or Pictures in PowerPoint, Word or Publisher

To change the size of a picture

Left click on the picture.

You will see buttons appear around the edge of the picture:

- the green circle button controls the angle of the picture
- the white circle buttons control the size.

Try moving your cursor onto the green button.

Your cursor has now changed to an arrowed circle.

Hold the left button down on your mouse and move it around.

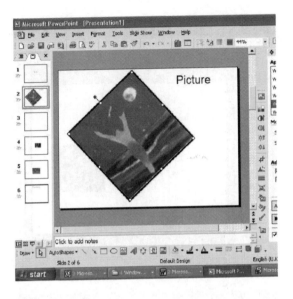

Now try the white buttons

When your cursor is in the right place it will change to arrows (when you hold down the left mouse button this will change to a cross).

You can now change the size by moving the mouse; when you have the correct size let go.

- The buttons (often referred to as 'handles') at the top and bottom make a picture longer.
- The buttons on the sides make a picture wider.
- The corner buttons move out horizontally and vertically at the same time (recommended for pictures of people so that they don't become distorted).

When you move the cursor into the middle of the picture it will change to an arrowed cross. You can then hold the left button down and move the picture around the screen.

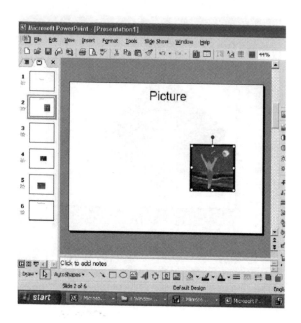

To crop a picture

Sometimes you may only want part of a picture. You can cut off parts of the picture, which is known as cropping.

You will need to use the 'Picture' toolbar (this should be showing in the bottom of your screen).

If this is not showing you will need to open it up.

Opening Toolbars

To open a toolbar left click on 'View'.

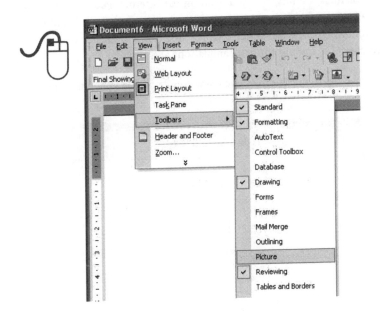

Move down to 'Toolbars' and across to the options (follow in line with the arrow).

Move down and left click on 'Picture'. The toolbar will then appear on your screen.

You now need to click on the picture to highlight it. Then click on the icon on the toolbar that looks like two crosses. You will notice that as you move the cursor over the edge of the picture the cursor will change.

Click on one of the 'handles' (the small squares in the corners and at the edge of the picture). Hold down the left mouse key and move towards the centre of the picture.

Once you release the mouse button the edge of the picture will have been 'cropped' (cut off).

Repeat the process if you would like to cut off other parts of the picture.

Helpsheet D: Using Google Search Engine

Google is one of many search engines which will help you to find the resources (information, pictures, sounds, etc.) you want on the Internet. People tend to have their own preferences for a search engine they use – you may have heard of Ask Jeeves or Yahoo! which are other search engines. However, Google is easy to use and is a great resource for finding pictures, animations and sounds.

If you are 'logged on' to the Internet type www.google.com in your address box and press 'Go'.

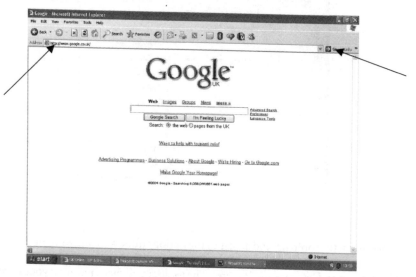

Note: If you want to look at websites in the UK only type www.google.co.uk in the address box.

Now you type in the 'keywords' of the information you want to research/find, for example you could type 'dogs'. This will list *all* the websites which have *anything* to do with dogs (this produced 38,600,000 sites).

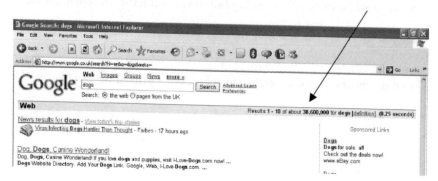

It is much better to 'refine' your search. That means typing in more specific information. When you want to look at dogs you usually want to know something specific such as 'dog breeders in the UK' or the type of dog (labrador, poodle, beagle) or 'dog trainers' or 'dog products', etc! If you type in more than one word Google will look for *both* of those words in the websites it lists.

To get pictures using Google

Google makes finding the right pictures easy. You may want a particular picture if you are illustrating a PowerPoint presentation or a person's lifestory or a poster for a forthcoming event. You will always be able to get a picture from the Internet.

This time when you go to the Google home page (i.e. you have typed www.google.com in the address box and pressed the 'Enter' key or clicked on 'Go') make sure you have selected 'Images' above the search box.

Now type in a type of dog (in this example I have typed 'Golden Retriever') and click on 'Google Search'. I have now got 42,100 pictures of golden retrievers to choose from!

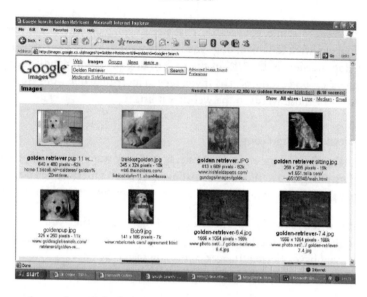

Once you have selected the picture you like you can 'Copy' it to the clipboard (so that you can 'Paste' it into any other programme you have open *or* 'Save' it to the hard drive or to a floppy disk in the usual way). To do this move the cursor over the picture you want and right click (i.e. click the right-hand mouse button). A new menu will appear:

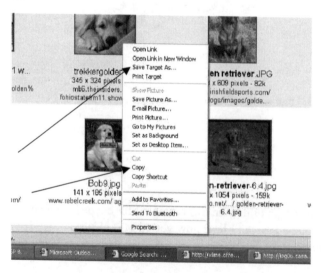

You can choose 'Save Target As…' and then you will be asked where you want to 'Save' the picture; or 'Copy' (which will copy it to the clipboard and you can then 'Paste' into a Word document or a PowerPoint slide).

Getting animations using Google

Google is also useful for finding animations (moving images) from the Internet. This time (still using Google Images) type 'dogs animated' and the following list will appear (or something similar):

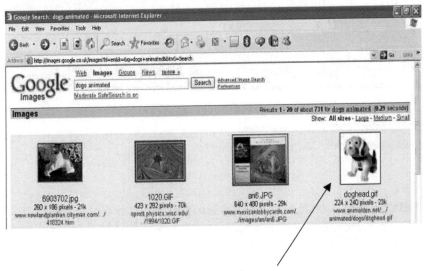

Animated pictures usually end in .gif, so look for those. In the example above, click on doghead.gif and a new screen will appear with the dog moving its head. You can copy this in the same way that you copied the picture above.

Note: Getting animations can be a bit hit-and-miss and you may have to try several before you can get one which works well!

Helpsheet E: WordArt

This is useful for creating headings or eye-catching text.

In Microsoft Word, open WordArt by clicking on this icon:

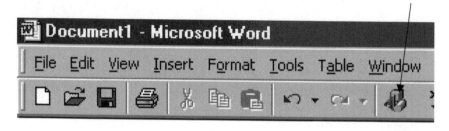

If this is not visible click on 'View', 'Toolbars' and 'Drawing'. This will open a toolbar which looks like this:

Click on this icon

A screen like this will appear:

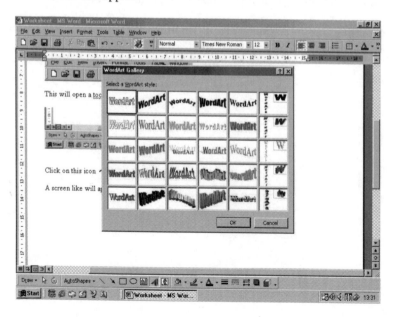

Now select the style you would like (by clicking on it). The following box will appear:

Type in the text which you want as your heading and click on 'OK'. Depending on the style you selected the heading will appear something like this:

Helpsheet F: Writing files to a CD

Using Windows XP

Windows XP has a feature already installed to record or 'burn' CDs.

To do this, right click on the folder or file you wish to save to a CD.

A menu of options will appear.

Scroll your mouse down to 'Send To'. Follow the arrow across for more options. Scroll down to the option that shows your CD writer and left click on this.

A speech balloon will appear at the bottom right of your screen. Left click in the balloon to continue.

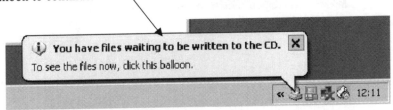

When you click on the balloon the following folder will appear.

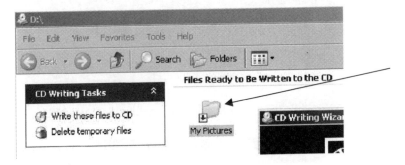

Left click once to highlight the chosen items to write to CD.

Next left click on 'Write these files to CD'. This will start up the CD Writing Wizard.

Left click on 'Next'.

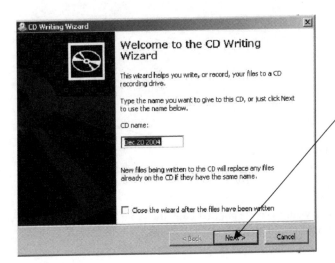

Insert a blank CD into the computer. Left click on 'Next'.

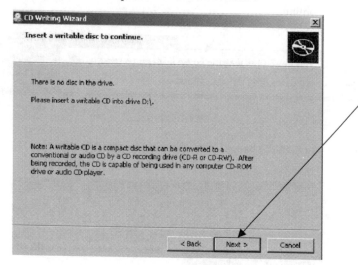

Now just wait while the computer copies everything onto your CD.

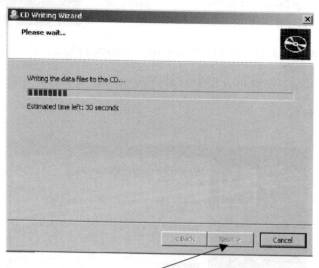

When completed, left click on 'Next'.
(While recording is in progress the next button will be greyed out so that you cannot action it.)

Note: If you want to create another copy the same as the first CD click your cursor into the box this will start the wizard again.

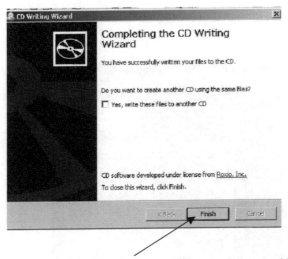

Your CD has now been created. Left click on the 'Finish' button (this will close down and complete the wizard).

Using Nero software

Nero is another industry standard programme which copies documents and files to CD-ROM or DVD.
Look for the 'Nero' icon.

This will either be a shortcut on your Desktop or within 'All Programs' ('Start'→ 'All Programs').

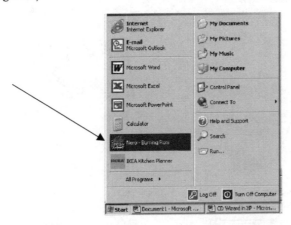

Left click on the 'Nero' icon to start. This will start the wizard.

Ensure that the 'CD' option is marked.
Left click on 'Next'.

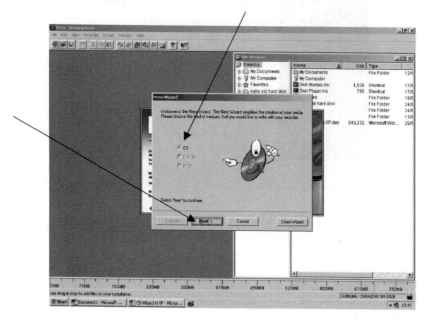

Ensure that the 'Compile a new CD' option is marked.
Left click on 'Next'.

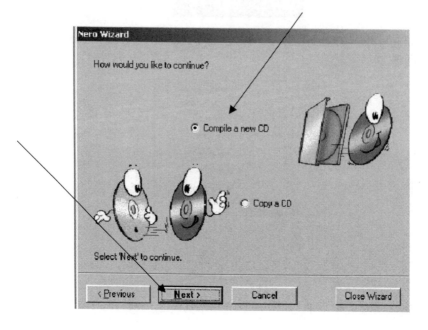

If you are copying files, folders or documents from your computer ensure that the 'Data CD' option is marked.

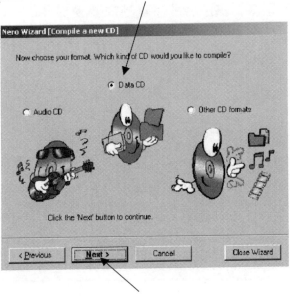

Then left click on 'Next'.

Choose which CD you are using. This would always be to create a new CD unless you are adding onto an existing re-writeable CD.

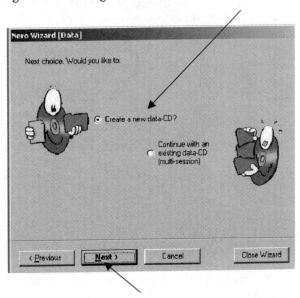

Then left click on 'Next'.

This next box is letting you know what to do next.

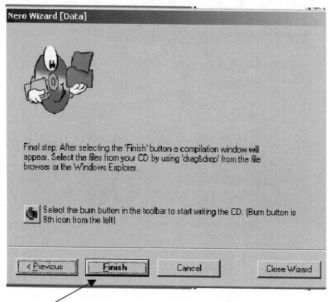

Left click on 'Finish' to proceed to the compilation section.

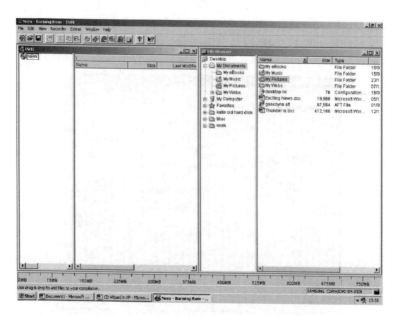

Drag the required items from either the third or fourth column into the second column ready for saving.

You can even copy and paste items in from other locations on your computer. When you have dragged everything you need into column two, left click on the 'Burn' icon.

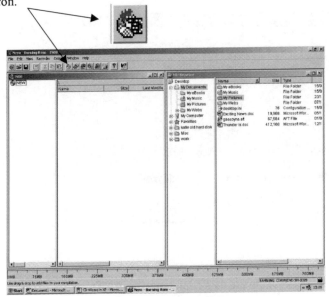

Note: At the bottom of the screen you can check to see how much room is left on the CD.

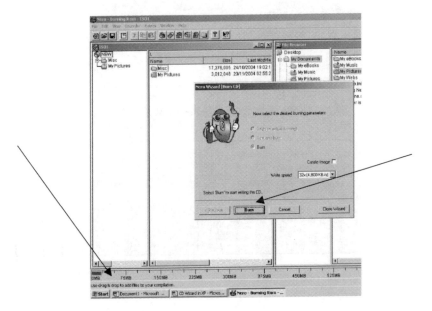

Left click on 'Burn'.

Insert your blank CD into the computer.

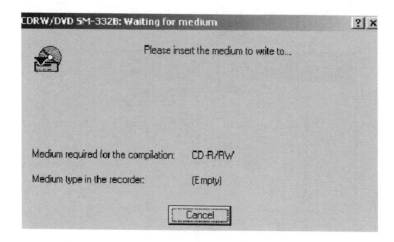

You can now wait while the data copies onto your CD.

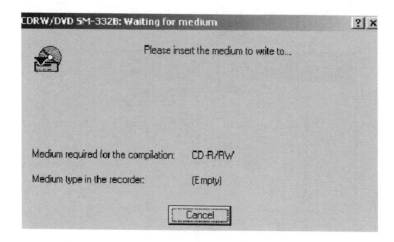

When it has completed it will bring up the option to 'Save', 'Print' or 'Discard' messages.

Left click on 'Discard'.

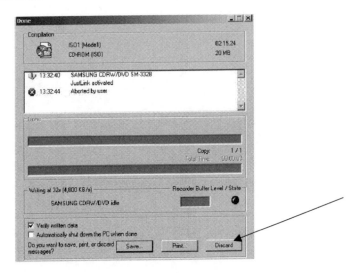

You will now go back to the compilation page.
Left click on the cross in the top right corner of the page.

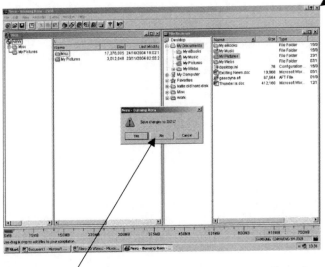

When asked to 'Save changes to…' select 'No' (unless you will need to copy this data to another CD).
The programme will now close.

Index